THE ESSENTIAL

Jewish Festival

COOKBOOK

Evelyn Rose

Robson Books

For Myer - always.

First published in Great Britain in 2000 by Robson Books, 10
Blenheim Court, Brewery Road, London N7 9NT

A member of the Chrysalis Group plc

British Library Cataloguing in Publication Data
A catalogue record for this title is available from the British Library

ISBN 1 86105 303 7

Photographs by Martin Brigdale
Designed and illustrated by Wladek Szechter
Printed in Spain.

Contents

Introduction

Our Jewish year is rich in Festivals both joyous and solemn, when we decorate our homes with fruit and flowers and bring our family and friends together in celebration. Inviting guests to share your table, and being invited out in turn is surely one of the most pleasant customs involved in being part of a Jewish community.

It is the 'minhagim' – the customs that have grown up round the Festivals during the centuries – that are so vital in giving us a sense of belonging and continuity, and it is food and its symbolism that has helped to ensure that these Festivals have remained central to Judaism throughout its history. Each generation has found dishes to help in the celebrations and the many table-centred rituals.

When Rosh Hashanah (the New Year) is drawing near, it's time to make the honeyed lekach and the apple pie and to buy in the spiral-shaped challah (enriched bread) which carries our hopes for a rich and round, sweet and fruitful year ahead.

Yom Kippur (the Day of Atonement) may be a Fast day, but there is a carefully chosen meal to be prepared beforehand and a light, digestible one afterwards. So a chicken dish to start the Fast and a plateful of tasty herring to break the Fast need to be prepared in good time.

Sukkot (Tabernacles) and Simchat Torah (the Rejoicing of the Law) are celebrated with vegetables stuffed to bursting with good things and with strudels both sweet and savoury celebrate the riches of the harvest, and in particular to mark the completion of the Torah Readings for the year, and the starting of the cycle yet again.

Hanukkah (the Festival of Lights) is a joyous festival and the miracle of the oil is marked with crispy latkes, sufganiyot (doughnuts) and other good things containing or cooked in oil.

Purim (the Feast of Lots) and the downfall of the wicked Haman means 'Hamantaschen' (Haman's pockets) stuffed with poppy seeds or other delights, and many triangular-shaped biscuits and other sweet things.

Then comes Pesach (Passover) when the whole house and in particular the kitchen are involved in celebrating the Israelites' escape from slavery. So there are great cook-ins, of flour-less cakes and biscuits, of home-made preserves, platefuls of fish both fried and stewed, and all without any trace of forbidden foods such as bread or flour.

Shavuot (the Feast of Weeks) brings dairy food on to our tables – blintzes and crispy cheese pancakes, cheesecakes both sweet and savoury – in celebration of the gift of the Torah (the Law) and the Ten Commandments.

I have written this book in the hope and expectation that it will help you to bring the wonderful culinary customs of the past into your way of living today. To survive, these customs must reflect the way we live now, not in the icy villages of Eastern Europe, but in warm homes. We don't need a fat-dominated diet to provide us with personal central heating; we don't have to rely on folk wisdom to plan a healthy diet. But we do need to treasure the family foods and customs we have inherited, so I have only modified, not completely revised the recipes. I have selected the finest of the traditional recipes and added to them many innovative ones which I hope will become the traditions of the future.

Liberated by modern technology from the culinary hard labour of the past, we are free now to glory in the remembered pleasures of the past, but also to teach new traditions to our children in the hope that they in turn will pass them on to their children.

The Jewish Year

Rosh Hashanah **1 and 2 Tishri**	New Year September/October
Yom Kippur	Day of Atonement 10 Tishri
Sukkot	Tabernacles September/October 15 Tishri
Simchat Torah	The Rejoicing of the Law 23 Tishri September/October
Hanukkah	Feast of Lights December 25 Kislev
Purim	Feast of Lots February/March 14 Adar
Pesach	Passover March/April 15 Nissan
Shavuot	Pentecost or Feast of Weeks May/June 6 Sivan

Food Storage Times

The recommended storage times given in the recipes are based on certain assumptions, as listed below

In the freezer

All foods, whether cooked or raw, are stored in airtight containers, freezer storage bags or foil packages, to prevent freezer 'burn'.

The exceptions are soft or fragile foods that are 'open frozen' until firm and must then be packaged in the same way.

The recommended storage time is based on the maximum period after which deterioration of flavour or texture may take place. If foods are frozen for longer than recommended, they will not be dangerous to eat but they will be past their prime.

In the refrigerator

All cooked and prepared foods are stored in airtight containers and covered with plastic wrap or foil to avoid dehydration and the transference of flavours and smells from one food to another.

All raw fruits and vegetables are stored in plastic bags or containers, according to variety.

The recommended storage time is based on the maximum period during which the food is pleasant and safe to eat.

Acknowledgements

In writing this book, I have been very fortunate in the help and support I have received from every one involved with it from conception to birth.

In the first place, it was the brain-child of my long-time publisher, Jeremy Robson, then Lorna Russell my literary editor, copy-editor Alison Leach together with publicity director Harriet Boston, helped it on its way with tremendous efficiency.

Rabbi Brian Fox, A.M., D.D. has been generous with his advice.

Nearer to home the production of the manuscript was yet again in the expert hands of my personal assistant Diane Ward whilst Christine Windeler kept the domestic infrastructure in excellent condition.

As with earlier books, this one could not have seen the light of day without the generosity of my family and friends who have not only given me great encouragement but also much practical help in sharing their treasured recipes. However, I take full responsibility for their present form, which took shape only after many tasting sessions in the kitchen and round the dinner table.

Above all, I cannot thank enough my ever-patient husband Myer for wrestling with the computer, checking the text with scrupulous care, and yet again sacrificing his waistline in his role of chief tester and taster.

Evelyn Rose
Manchester, England
January 2000

Festival Classics

Once upon a time, a generation or two ago, there was a particular list of dishes that spelled 'Shabbat'. These were the ones that not only had a very special flavour and richness in honour of Shabbat (such as chicken soup, knaidlach and fish in its many manifestations), but were also particularly suitable to make on the Eve of Shabbat, still tasting good – or even better – when eaten a day or two later. So Thursday and Friday were devoted to 'making Shabbat' so that the injunction to avoid cooking on that day could be followed to the letter.

There are still some households where this 'minhag' (custom) of preparing traditional dishes is followed every week, but many more cook these dishes only for Festivals – any Festival. In this chapter, therefore, I have gathered together some of the best of these dishes – traditional chicken soup, knaidlach and classic chopped fried fish amongst others – for handy reference. However, I have suggested making them using the latest technology, where possible. For instance, Gefilte Fish Provençal is cooked in the microwave, being a recipe that works particularly well when prepared this way. It has to be said this is not the case with the majority of traditional dishes – such as chicken soup – which need long slow simmering to be enjoyed at their best.

I have included a delicious light fruit cake which would be welcome on any Yomtov table, but which is made so quickly that it can be fitted into even the most demanding life style. I have also given a lekach recipe, as there is an old tradition that it should be eaten on any Yomtov, not just at Rosh Hashanah. It's a very good-tempered cake which actually comes to life when it is allowed a few days to 'mature' after baking. In the Rosh Hashanah chapter there is another lekach that is large enough to be cut into 48 generous pieces! (See p.32)

Kreplach (Jewish ravioli) were once a feature of all three Harvest Festivals – Pesach, Shavuot and Sukkot, as their three-cornered shape was said to symbolize the three Patriarchs – Abraham, Isaac and Jacob. I must confess that it's only for the meal before the Yom Kippur Fast that I indulge in this time-consuming preparation.

I cannot pretend that making 'chrane' (beetroot and horseradish sauce) is a weekly chore in our house, but my husband saw it as a challenge and the result was so good that whenever chopped fried fish or traditional fried fish is on a Yomtov menu, the cry goes up 'Dad, what about making some chrane?' It's so good, and so easy to make with ready-grated horseradish. But if you are tempted to grate the horseradish yourself, be warned – your eyes will be streaming!

Myer's Home-Made Chrane

Serves 10 (approx.)

Keeps up to 2 weeks in the refrigerator.

150g (5oz/3 heaped tbsp)
ready-grated horseradish
from jar (English
Provender Company)
2 medium cooked beetroot
(not in vinegar), 5cm
(2″) in diameter
2 tbsp wine vinegar or
cider vinegar
2 tsp sugar
1 tsp salt

This is just right in strength – neither will it blow your head off nor taste like a bland beetroot purée. Using ready-grated horse-radish, it is made in minutes.

1. Put the grated horseradish in a small bowl. Grate in the beetroot, then mix thoroughly until evenly pink. Add the vinegar to make a spoonable mixture, then add sugar and salt.

2. Taste for seasoning and add more vinegar, sugar or salt to taste.

3. Put in a screw-top jar and refrigerate.

Chrane

It was called 'Sauce Raifort' on the menu, but it was definitely chrane that I was served with my 'Quenelles de Brochet' (pike fish dumplings) in the village inn at Eguisheim on the Route du Vin in Alsace.

So how did this traditional Eastern European Jewish mixture of grated horseradish and beetroot find its way to my plate? Is it too fanciful to con-jecture that it was first taken east from Alsace with the Jews who migrat-ed from there to Russia and Poland in the late Middle Ages?

Whatever its origin, there is nothing to equal chrane as an accompani-ment to 'chopped and fried' and plain fried fish. Chrane is now produced in factories, but providing you can buy the horseradish ready-grated, there's nothing to equal the home-made variety!

Traditional Chicken Soup

Serves 6–8 (photograph between pages 56 and 57)

Keeps 3 days in the refrigerator. Freeze 3 months. An essential for any Festival!

1. Put the fowl wings and giblets (but not the liver) in a large heavy soup pan with the water and the salt and pepper. Break up the carcasses (if used) and add to the pan. Cover and bring to the boil. Remove any froth with a large, wet metal spoon.

2. Peel the onion and carrots. Cut in half and add to the pan together with the celery and parsley.

3, Bring back to the boil, then reduce the heat so that the liquid is barely bubbling. Cover and continue to simmer for a further 3 hours, either on top of the stove or in a slow oven, 150°C (300°F/Gas 2) or until the fowl feels very tender when a leg is prodded.

4. Strain the soup into a large bowl. Discard the vegetables and carcasses (if used). Cover the soup and put in the refrigerator overnight. Refrigerate or freeze the fowl for later use.

5. Next day, remove any congealed fat and return the soup to the pan. If there is a thick layer of fat, it can be heated in a pan to drive off any liquid. When it has stopped bubbling, it can be cooled and stored like rendered raw fat in the refrigerator.

6. Add the cubes of carrot and the shreds of leek to the soup, and simmer for 15 minutes. Taste and strengthen the flavour, if necessary, with one or two chicken stock cubes

7. Serve with a soup garnish such as lokshen, allow approximately 15g (½oz) per person cooked in boiling water or in the soup), knaidlach (see pages 4-5) or kreplach (see p. 6).

a whole or half fowl,
with wings and giblets
  (if available)
1 or 2 roast chicked car-
  casses (if available)
1.75 litres (3 pints/7½
  cups) water
2 tsp salt
pinch of white pepper
1 or 2 roast chicken car-
  casses (if available)
1 large onion
2 large carrots
leaves and top 5cm (2″) of
  2 sticks celery
1 sprig parsley

To add the next day:
1 large carrot, cut in tiny
  cubes
5cm (2″) white part of a
  leek, finely sliced

Traditional Chicken Soup

Ever since, some years ago, chicken soup was first called 'Jewish Penicillin' it has become the most publicized soup in the world! All kinds of medicinal properties have been ascribed to it, and claims for its curative power have encompassed almost every human complaint, whether in babyhood or old age!

Knaidlach

Serves 6–8

Keeps 2 days in the refrigerator. Freeze 1 month.

2 large eggs
2 very slightly rounded
   tbsp rendered chicken
   fat, chicken-flavoured
   vegetable fat or soft
   margerine
5 tbsp warm chicken soup
   or water
1 tsp salt
$\frac{1}{4}$ tsp white pepper
1oz ($\frac{1}{4}$ cup) ground
   almonds
125g (4oz/1 cup) medium
   matzah meal

This is my definitive recipe which results in perfect soup 'dumplings' every time.

1. Whisk the eggs until fluffy, then stir in the soft fat, soup or water, seasonings, ground almonds and matzah meal, and mix thoroughly. The mixture should look moist and thick, and should not be quite firm enough to form into balls. If too soft, add a little more meal; if too firm, add a teaspoon or two of water.

2. Chill for at least an hour, but overnight will do no harm. The mixture will then firm up.

3. Half-fill a pan with water and bring to the boil, then add 2 teaspoons of salt. Take pieces of the chilled mixture the size of large walnuts and roll between wetted palms into balls.

4. Drop these balls into the boiling water. Reduce the heat until the water is simmering, then cover and simmer for 40 minutes without removing the lid.

5. Strain the balls with a slotted spoon and drop into simmering chicken soup.

Knaidlach

Matzah balls or 'halkes' are other names given to these spongy soup dumplings. Every experienced Jewish cook is confident that her recipe is the original and best! However, for the benefit of the inexperienced, here is what I consider to be the definitive recipe. I suggest you first try my recipe as it is, then according to the texture favoured by your family, adjust the quantities of matzah meal or water.

Open-freeze the cooked and drained knaidlach until solid – about 2 hours – then put them into plastic bags. To use, defrost for 1 hour at room temperature, then reheat in the simmering soup.

For a smaller number, or for a special occasion, cook the knaidlach in chicken soup rather than in water. They will absorb some of the soup and with it, its delicious flavours.

Light Knaidlach

Serves 6 (approx.)

Keeps 2 days in the refrigerator. Freeze 1 month.

Light and fluffy, these may not have quite the flavour of traditional knaidlach made with chicken fat and ground almonds, but they're still delicious in their own right.

125g (4oz/1 cup) medium matzah meal
225 ml (8 floz/1 cup) boiling water
1 large egg whisked until frothy
2 tbsp vegetable oil
1 tsp salt
speck of white pepper

1. Put the matzah meal into a bowl and stir in the boiling water, followed by all the other ingredients. Mix thoroughly, then refrigerate for 1 hour to allow the matzah meal to swell and the mixture to firm up.

2. Have ready a large pan of boiling water containing 2 teaspoons of salt.

3. Roll the mixture into little balls about the size of walnuts.

4. Drop into the boiling water and then simmer uncovered for about 20 minutes, or until the knaidlach rise to the top of the pan. Drain, then put into simmering chicken soup.

Kreplach

Makes 48 (approx.)

Keep for 3 days cooked or 1 day raw in the refrigerator. Freeze cooked for 3 months.

For the dough:
225g (8oz/2 cups) plain (all-purpose) flour
pinch of salt
2 eggs
1 tbsp + 2 tsp lukewarm water

For the filling:
½ medium onion, peeled and cut into 2.5-9cm (1-inch) chunks
350g (12oz) shin beef, cooked and cut into 2.5cm (1-inch) chunks
1 egg
½ level tsp salt
pinch of white pepper

Kreplach can be cooked in either boiling salted water or in chicken soup.

The labour of love involved in making 'Jewish ravioli' by hand has been transformed by the advent of the electric mixer and the food processor.

Using a mixer:
1. Put the flour and salt in a bowl, then make a well and add the eggs and water.

2. Knead with the dough hook until a smooth, non-sticky dough is formed (3–4 minutes).

Using a food processor:
1. With the metal blade, process the flour, eggs and salt until thoroughly blended.

2. Slowly add the water through the feed tube until the mixture forms a ball that leaves the sides of the bowl clear.

3. If the dough is too sticky (it will depend on the absorbency quality of the flour), add a little more flour.

4. Process for a further 40 seconds to knead the dough.

Using either method:
5. Turn the dough out on to a floured board.

6. Knead briefly with the heel of the hand to ensure that the dough looks like chamois leather – that is, very smooth and springy.

7. Cover with a large bowl and leave to 'relax' for 20 minutes.

To make the filling
8. Pulse the onion and meat in the food processor until finely

'minced' – after about 5 seconds. Do not process until pasty.

9. Add the egg and seasonings through the feed tube.

10. Process until evenly moistened and just beginning to cling together – another 3 seconds. Alternatively, put the onion and meat through the mincer, then stir in the beaten egg and seasonings.

11. Turn into a bowl.

12. To shape the kreplach: for easier handling, divide the dough into four.

13. Roll each piece until it is paper thin and you can see the board through it. It will then be about 35cm (14″) square – if sufficiently kneaded, it will not stick to the board.

14. Have ready a very large pan full of boiling salted water or chicken soup.

15. Cut the dough into pieces 5cm (2″) square.

16. Put a teaspoon of the meat filling in the centre of each square, then fold over into a triangle, pressing the edges securely to seal – dampen them with water only if necessary.

17. As each kreplach is formed, lay it on a sheet of greaseproof (wax) paper.

18. Add one-third of the kreplach to the pan and bring back to the boil.

19. Cover and cook for 15 minutes, tasting after 10 minutes to see if they are tender.

20. Drain and reserve.

21. Repeat with the remaining kreplach.

22. Alternatively, the uncooked kreplach can be left out in the kitchen until quite dry – after about 2 hours (turning once or twice). Then refrigerate and cook as required.

23. Reheat the cooked kreplach in the soup for 10–15 minutes.

Classic Chopped Fried Fish

Makes 12–14 patties (for 36–40 see larger quantities)

Keeps 3 days in the refrigerator. Freeze 3 months raw or cooked. Serve at room temperature, not immediately after frying.

For 12–14 patties:
1 medium onion, peeled
2 eggs
2 tsp sugar
2 tsp salt
pinch of white pepper
1 tbsp oil
50g (2oz/½ cup)
  medium matzah meal
450g (1 lb)
  haddock fillet, skinned
450g (1 lb)
  cod fillet, skinned

For 36–40 patties:
450g (1 lb) onion, peeled
6 eggs
6 tsp sugar
6 tsp salt
¼ tsp white pepper
3 tbsp oil
175g (6oz/1½ cups)
  medium matzah meal
1.3kg (2¾ lb)
  haddock fillet, skinned
1.3kg (2¾ lb)
  cod fillet, skinned

For coating:
dry breadcrumbs or
  matzah meal

For Festivals, it's worth preparing the larger amount as the patties freeze to perfection either cooked or raw.

1. Cut the onion into 2.5cm (1″) chunks and put into a food processor. Add the eggs, sugar, seasonings and oil, then process until reduced to a smooth purée. (If you wish to make a larger quantity but are using a standard size processor, you will need to do this in two batches.)

2. Pour this purée into a large bowl and stir in the matzah meal, then leave to swell for 10 minutes.

3. If possible get the fishmonger to mince the fish. Otherwise cut the fish into 2.5cm (1″) chunks and put in the processor, half-filling the bowl each time.

4. Process for 5 seconds, until the fish is finely chopped, but before it is reduced to a purée.

5. Add to the meal mixture and blend in using a large fork. Mix thoroughly – if preparing a large quantity, this is most easily done with the widespread fingers of one hand. The mixture should be firm enough to shape into a soft patty or ball. If it feels too cloggy, rinse out the processor bowl with a tablespoon or two of water and stir that in. If it feels very soft, stir in a tablespoon or two of meal.

6. Leave for 30 minutes, or refrigerate overnight.

To shape into patties or balls:
7. Dip your hands into cold water and form the mixture into patties about 7cm (2¾″) long, 4cm wide (1½″) and 2cm (¾ inch) thick, or into balls the size of a small apple. The fish can now be cooked or frozen raw; do not coat at this stage as the coating will go soggy in the freezer.

To freeze raw:
8. Arrange the patties or balls side by side on a tray lined with

greaseproof (wax) paper or foil. When the tray is full, cover with a layer of paper or foil and make another layer on top.

9. Put the tray, uncovered, in the freezer for 2 hours or until the patties are firm to the touch. They can now be packed, 12 into a plastic bag, or they can be individually wrapped in clingfilm (plastic wrap) to make it easy to remove a few at a time.

To defrost:
10. Lay the frozen patties side by side on a board. Leave overnight in the refrigerator, or from 1 to 3 hours at room temperature, until they are soft all the way through. They can now be coated with matzah meal or breadcrumbs, and treated as if newly pre-pared. Alternatively, the uncoated balls or patties can be used to make Gefilte Fish Provençale.(see p. 12)

To freeze cooked patties:
11. Allow the patties to cool completely, then wrap each one sepa-rately in clingfilm (plastic wrap) and store in plastic bags.

To thaw, reheat and recrisp cooked patties:
12. Remove the clingfilm (plastic wrap) and arrange the frozen pat-ties on a baking tray. Reheat at 180°C (350°F/Gas 4) until crisp to the touch – after about 15 minutes. Allow to cool before serving.

To fry the patties:
13. This is most easily done in a deep-fryer, but you can use a deep frying pan. In either case, coat the patties evenly, either with fine dry breadcrumbs (easily prepared on the food processor from dry stale challah), or a 50/50 mix of fine and medium matzah meal.

> ## Classic Chopped Fried Fish
>
> This method of cooking gefilte fish surely entitles it to be a candidate for the very first convenience food – on a par with the sandwich and the Cornish pasty! Some years ago, a parcel of patties was taken on a school trip by rail to Moscow, and the fish was the only food still edible after three days! (A test, however, not to be recommended as a general rule.)
>
> This long 'shelf' life is entirely due to the use of oil rather than a solid fat as the cooking medium. Oil does not congeal when it cools, so although the fish is undoubt-edly at its best the day it is cooked, the just-fried crispness can be restored by a few min-utes in a moderate oven, until the patties are crisp to the touch.
>
> My favourite frying medi-um is groundnut (peanut) oil (much favoured also by many professional chefs), but every flavourless oil has its champions!

To use a deep-fryer:
14. Remove the basket, then heat the oil to 190°C (375°F). Cook 5 or 6 patties at a time, for 6–7 minutes or until a rich golden-brown.

To use a frying pan:
15. Heat oil 2.5cm (1″) deep until it is hot enough to brown a 2.5cm (1-inch) cube of bread in 30 seconds.

16. Gently lower in enough balls to fill the pan without overcrowding it – usually 5 or 6 in a 22.5cm (9″) pan. Cook steadily over a moderate heat, turning every 2 or 3 minutes, until the patties are an even brown, 7 or 8 minutes in all.

17. In either case, lift out with a slotted spoon and drain the fish by standing it up round the sides of a dish lined with crumpled kitchen or tissue paper.

18 Serve with salads, baked potatoes or chrane (see p. 2).

Fish Steaks or Fillets Fried in the Jewish Style

Serves 6–8

Keeps 2 days lightly covered in the refrigerator. Freeze 3 months.
The ideal method for keeping fried fish edible for more than one day.

6–8 fillets
  or steaks of fish
salt
2 eggs
2 rounded tbsp plain
  (all-purpose) flour
coating crumbs or matzah
  meal, approx. 175g
  (6oz/1½ cups) depending
  on the size of the fish
  steaks or fillets

Steaks of sole, haddock, cod, halibut or large plaice should be cut 2–2.5cm (¾–1″) thick. Fillets should be 2.5cm (1″) thick. Fillets of plaice, sole or baby halibut should be cut from fish not less than 675g (1½ lb) in weight.

1. Wash the fish under cold running water and arrange round the sides of a colander. Sprinkle lightly with cooking salt and leave to drain.

2. To coat the fish, have ready 3 shallow plastic or glass containers, each slightly longer than the fillet or steak of fish. Arrange these containers side by side, with flour in one, beaten egg in the second and dried coating crumbs (the colour of oatmeal) or matzah meal in the third. Stale challah or French bread which has been allowed to dry out completely in the bread bin or drawer can be crushed to crumbs in the food processor.

3. Dip the washed and drained fish into the flour, patting off any excess. Then dip into the egg, spreading it in an even layer all over the surface of the fish with a pastry brush, and finally dip them into the crumbs, patting them on in an even layer. Arrange the coated fish on a tray ready for frying.

To fry using a deep-fryer:
4. Remove the frying basket as this increases the capacity of the pan.

5. Pour in the oil to the depth recommended by the manufacturer, then heat the oil to 190°C (375°F).

6. It is essential not to crowd the pan, as too much cold fish can drastically lower the temperature of the oil and so allow the fish to absorb it before the temperature can be restored.

7. Close the pan and set the timer for 7 minutes for fillets, 8 minutes for steaks.

8. While the fish is cooking, line a shallow casserole with crumpled paper towels or tissue paper. When the fish is a rich brown, lift it out with a large slotted spoon and lay it on its side round the edge of the dish so that any drops of free oil can drain away. After 5–6 minutes (just before the next batch is ready) the fish can be lifted carefully on to a serving dish.

To fry by the traditional method:
9. Choose a heavy-based frying pan with sides at least 5cm (2") high and at least 22.5–30cm (9–12") in diameter.

10. Heat the empty pan for 3 minutes over medium heat, then put the oil into it to a depth of 2.5cm (1 inch) and heat steadily for 4 minutes. Test to see that a cube of bread browns in 30 seconds or an oil thermometer registers 190°C (375°F).

11. Lift up the fish on a slotted spoon and lower it into the hot oil. Do not overcrowd the pan; too much cold fish put in too soon will lower the temperature drastically and the fish will be soggy.

12. Cook the fish over medium heat with the oil bubbling steadily, until the first side is a rich brown – about 4 minutes for a fillet, 5–7 minutes for a thick steak.

13. Turn it carefully using a slotted spoon and a fork, and cook until the second side is brown.

14. Have ready a shallow casserole or a cooling tray covered with crumpled kitchen paper. Lift out the fish to drain.

With either method:
15. If the fillets are not stiff and crisp when they are lifted out, turn up the heat and return them to the pan for a further minute's cooking in the hot oil. Perfect fried fish should look dry and crisp.

16. As soon as the fish has drained completely, lift it on to a platter and store until required.

Gefilte Fish Provençale in the Microwave

Serves 4–6

Keeps 4 days in the refrigerator. Freeze 3 months.

8–9 fish patties (total
  weight approx.
  900 g/2 lb) (see Chopped
  Fried Fish, p. 8)

For the sauce:
1 can or tube tomato
  purée or 2 rounded tbsp,
  or 1 x 190g jar sun-dried
  tomato paste
300 ml (10 floz/1¼ cups)
  boiling water
2 tsp olive or sunflower oil
1 level tbsp minced
  dried onion
2 canned sweet red pep-
  pers, drained and cut in
  thin strips, or 1 large red
  pepper (bell pepper),
  cut in strips
1 tbsp tomato ketchup
1 bay leaf
10 grinds of black pepper
1 tsp dried Italian herbs
  or herbes de Provence
1 tsp brown sugar

The microwave really comes into its own when used to cook this superbly flavoured dish – best eaten the day after preparation.

1. Whisk all the sauce ingredients together until smooth in a 1.2-litre (2-pint/5-cup) microwave-safe jug or bowl. Heat the sauce, covered, on 100 per cent power for 3 minutes.

2. Arrange the raw patties side by side in a casserole. Pour over the sauce, and cook covered on 100 per cent power for 6 minutes. Remove the lid, baste the fish with the sauce, then re-cover and cook on 50 per cent power for a further 5 minutes.

3. Leave covered for 10 minutes, then cool and refrigerate until required. Leave at room temperature for 1 hour before serving.

Yomtov Light Fruit Cake

Keeps 3 weeks in an airtight container. Freeze 6 months.

Light but fruitful, the mixed spice adds a distinctive taste to this simple cake. It looks most impressive baked in a long slim loaf tin (mine is 30 x 12 x 7.5cm /12 x 4½ x 3″ deep), though it also looks good in a 20cm (8″) round tin, 7.5cm (3″) deep. If you can resist the temptation, leave it for 2 days before cutting.

1. Preheat the oven to 180°C (350°F/Gas 4). Brush the chosen tin with oil and line the base with a strip or circle of silicone or greaseproof (wax) paper.

2. In a food processor, process the eggs and sugar for 2 minutes, then drop in spoonfuls of the fat and pulse until it disappears (don't worry if the mixture looks curdled).

3. Add the flour, baking powder, lemon rind, spice and liquid and pulse 12 times until the mixture is smooth and evenly blended. Clean down the sides, then add the nuts and pulse twice. Add the dried fruit and pulse twice more.

4. Turn into the chosen tin and smooth level. Brush lightly with the milk or water and scatter lightly with the sugar. Arrange the reserved nuts on top.

5. Bake for 30 minutes then reduce the temperature to 160°C (325°F/Gas 3) and cook for a further 35 minutes (for the loaf) or 45 minutes (for the round cake) until the top is firm to the touch and a skewer comes out clean from the centre.

6. Cool on a rack, then wrap well in foil and store in a plastic container or bag.

3 eggs
175g (6oz/¾ cup) light or medium Muscovado (soft brown) sugar
175g (6oz/¾ cup) soft butter or margarine
225g (8oz/2 cups) plain (all-purpose) flour with 1 level tsp baking powder
finely-grated rind of 1 lemon
2 tsp mixed spice
2 tbsp milk or water
100g (4oz/1 cup) pack pecans or walnut halves, coarsely chopped (reserve 8 halves)
225g (8oz/1½ cups) mixed dried fruit
oil for brushing the tin

For the glaze:
a little milk or water
demerara sugar
the 8 reserved pecans or walnut halves

Classic Lekach

Keeps 2 weeks at room temperature in an airtight container. Freeze 3 months.

175g (6oz/1½ cups) plain
   (all-purpose) flour
75g (3oz/⅓ cup)
   caster (superfine) sugar
½ tsp ground ginger
½ tsp ground cinnamon
1 level tsp ground mixed
   spice
225g (8oz/¾ cup)
   clear honey
4 tbsp sunflower oil
grated rind of 1 orange
2 eggs
1 level tsp bicarbonate of
   soda (baking soda)
75 ml (3 floz/⅓ cup)
   orange juice

The flavour and the texture of this cake need a few days to reach moist perfection.

1. Preheat the oven to 180°C (350°F/Gas 4). Line a cake tin 25 x 20 x 5cm (10 x 8 x 2″) with silicone or greaseproof (wax) paper. (It is vital to use a tin of this exact size as the cake rises considerably as it bakes).

2. Mix together the flour, sugar and spices.

3. Make a well in the centre, then add the honey, oil, orange rind and eggs. Beat well until smooth.

4. Dissolve the bicarbonate of soda in the orange juice. Stir into the flour mixture. The mixture will now be very thin.

5. Pour into the tin and bake for 50–55 minutes, or until firm to the touch.

6. Remove from the oven and leave to cool. When quite cold, wrap in foil and leave at room temperature, if possible for 4–5 days before using.

Classic Lekach

Lekach, the archetypal cake for Rosh Hashanah, is usually translated as 'honey cake' because honey was the most widely available sweetener in earlier times. Sugar was considered a luxury until the end of the 19th century and in Britain at least was sold – like medicine – at the chemist's! However, the Yiddish word simply means any special cake baked for a Yomtov or Simcha (celebration). According to a Lubavitch cookery book, one should always eat at least an ounce of this type of sweet cake when drinking the wine after Kiddush – it's the sweetness that counts!

Rosh Hashanah
The New Year

The scent of autumn flowers, the perfume of melon, the brightness of pome-granates – Rosh Hashanah may herald the start of the 'Days of Awe', the Ten Days of Penitence, culminating in the Fast of Yom Kippur, but it is still a joy-ous Festival in the home, with bouquets of flowers and plants exchanged between family and friends and a host of time-honoured dishes to be enjoyed, both in the making and at the dinner table.

'Tradition, tradition!' That best describes the foods that appear on our Rosh Hashanah tables each year. In both Ashkenazi and Sephardi households, dishes containing honey, apples, exotic fruits, carrots, fish and seeds of all kinds carry our hopes for a New Year that will be rich in sweetness, fruitfulness and fulfilment in the months ahead. There is no shortage of dishes expressing roundness, sweetness and continuity through the different generations.

The concept of sweetness as a harbinger of good fortune is thought to have originated in the fifth century BCE. Ever since the return from Babylon, it has been introduced in dishes by using dried fruits and honey as in the Ashkenazi Pflaumen Tsimmes, the Sephardi M'Rouzya Tagine, and the honey-rich spiced Lekach cake.

While all kinds of fruits are served at Rosh Hashanah, the apple is the symbol-ic food of the season, expressing in both its sweetness and its round shape our hopes for a happy and fulfilling New Year. Used in all kinds of pies such as the Filo Pastry Tarte with a Caramelized Apple Filling and puddings such as the Apple and Ginger Lekach, it is also served dipped in honey in both Ashkenazi and Sephardi households after Kiddush (the prayer of sanctification) has been recited on the Eve of the Festival. On the second night it is the custom to serve an infrequently eaten fruit such as the pomegranate and to recite the Blessing which is always said over a new and fresh food.

As at every other Festival, no table is complete without a dish of fish – fried steaks or fillets (see p. 10) or Gefilte fish in some form (see pages 8 and 12). Chicken dishes such as Chicken Breasts with Roasted Lemons or Succulent Roast Chicken are always on the menu, and cakes and biscuits such as the Fluffy Chocolate Fingers and Almond Butter Crisps are served at family tea parties.

At every Jewish baker's, the challot (enriched bread) takes on a spiral instead of a plaited shape, and is often enriched with extra eggs, honey and raisins. If you are familiar with yeast cooking, there's an extra delight to be found in baking two of these loaves yourself.

I have included in this section more innovative dishes – such as Butternut Squash Soup, Shoulder of Lamb with an Apricot and Pine Kernel Stuffing and Salmon Steaks with an Avocado Salsa, which may well become symbolic traditions in the twenty-first century.

Crunchy Glazed Nuts

These will keep at least a month if you can resist them. You may wish to use cinnamon instead of the curry powder.

2 egg whites
2 tbsp caster (superfine)
  sugar
1 tbsp mild curry powder
225g (8oz/2 cups) whole
  blanched almonds
175g (6oz/1½ cups) cashew
  nuts
50g (2oz/¼ cup) pistachio
  nuts or hazel nuts

1. Preheat the oven to 160°C (325°F/Gas 3).

2. Whisk the egg whites to soft peaks, then whisk in the sugar and curry powder (the mixture will be of coating consistency).

3. Fold in the nuts, then spread on a baking sheet lined with silicone paper or Teflon liner.

4. Bake for 30–35 minutes, shaking and turning the nuts every 10 minutes until they are a rich golden brown. They crispen as they cool.

5. Leave to cool, then store in an airtight tin.

Mango, Melon & Lime Cocktail

Serves 8

The marinated melon and mango make a particularly colourful combination, and together they make a refreshing start to a meal.

1. Peel the mango and cut in neat segments.

2. Chill the segments overnight in the lime juice sweetened with the sugar. (This has a magical effect on the taste and texture of the fruit.)

3. Scoop balls or cubes out of the melons and refrigerate.

4. An hour or two before dinner, drain off and discard any juice from the melons, then combine the two fruits.

5. Divide between small glasses or bowls and garnish with the mint.

1 very large or 2 medium
  fully ripe mangoes
juice of 1 large lime
2 tbsp caster (superfine)
  sugar
1 very large or 2 medium
  Galia or Ogen melons

For the garnish:
tiny sprigs of mint

Chicken-Liver Pâté with a taste Of China

Serves 8 plus leftovers

Keeps 5 days in the refrigerator. Freeze 1 month.

4 hard-boiled eggs
5 level tbsp rendered
  chicken fat
1 large onion, peeled and
  finely chopped
1 large clove of garlic,
  peeled and finely
  chopped
2 tbsp finely chopped
  peeled ginger
1 tsp sea salt
20 grinds of black pepper
$\frac{1}{4}$ tsp ground nutmeg
450g (1 lb) chicken livers,
  koshered and halved
3 tbsp brandy
2 rounded tbsp ginger
  slivers

My favourite 'chopped' liver, smooth as silk on the tongue. The ginger adds extra zing in honour of the New Year.

1. Boil the eggs for 10 minutes, then drench with cold water and leave.

2. Sauté the onion in the fat until beginning to caramelize, then add the garlic and ginger and continue to cook for a further 2–3 minutes until a pleasant aroma arises.

3. Sprinkle with the seasonings, then add the halved koshered livers and toss gently to absorb the flavours in the pan.

4. Pour the brandy into the pan and allow to bubble until it has almost evaporated.

5. Turn into a food processor, together with the shelled and halved eggs, and process until absolutely smooth, cleaning down the sides of the bowl as necessary.

6. Turn into a bowl, cover and leave refrigerated for several hours for the flavours to develop. One hour before using, leave at room temperature.

7. Meanwhile, fry the ginger slivers in a little hot oil. Drain on paper towels, then set aside.

8. The pâté can now be served in little pots or an entrée dish. Spike the top with the ginger slivers. Serve with slices or fingers of fresh or toasted challah.

Butternut Squash & Apple Soup

Serves 6–8 (photograph between pages 56 and 57)

Keeps 3 days in the refrigerator. Freeze 2 months.

Fruity and slightly sweet, this is the perfect 'symbolic' soup for this Festival of sweet and fruity foods.

1. Peel the squash with a swivel-bladed peeler. Cut in half and remove seeds. Thinly slice the onion and the peeled and seeded squash (easiest in a food processor).

2. Put the onions, salt, white pepper and oil in a soup pan. Cover and cook over moderate heat for 5 minutes until the onions have softened. Uncover and continue to cook for another few minutes until they are a golden colour, adding the 2 tablespoons apple juice and stirring well with a wooden spoon to stop them sticking to the pan.

3. Now add the sliced squash and the hot stock with the 1 teaspoon salt and the black pepper. Cover and cook gently for 20–30 minutes until the squash is tender when pierced with a pointed knife.

4. Allow to cool for 20 minutes before puréeing until absolutely smooth in a blender or food processor.

5. Meanwhile, peel, core and thinly slice the apples.

6. Melt the butter or margarine in a small pan. Add the apples and sauté them for a few minutes, stirring all the time until they are heated through and have absorbed the fat.

7. Now add the apple juice and stir well. Cover and cook until soft – about 8 minutes. Uncover and cook until thick and juicy.

8. Mash with a fork to a purée, then stir this apple mixture into the soup. Taste and re-season.

9. To serve, reheat the soup until simmering.

1kg (2¼ lb) butternut or buttercup (kabocha) squash
1 x 225g (8oz) onion, peeled
½ tsp salt
pinch of white pepper
1 tbsp sunflower or olive oil
2 tbsp apple juice
1.4 litres (2½ pints) hot vegetable stock
1 tsp salt
20 grinds of black pepper

For the apple mixture:
2 eating apples, e.g. Golden Delicious
1 tbsp butter or margarine
125 ml (4 floz/½ cup) apple juice

Grilled or Baked Salmon Steaks with an Avocado Salsa

Serves 6–8 (photograph between pages 56 and 57)

Leftover salmon keeps 2 days in the refrigerator, the avocado salsa for 1 day.

6–8 steaks of salmon, each
175g (6oz) in weight and
2cm (¾ inch) thick
fine sea salt and freshly
ground black pepper
60–75g (2½–3oz/¾ stick) butter
a little flour for dredging the
fish
40–50g (1½–2oz/⅓ cup) flaked
almonds
3 tbsp lemon juice

For the Avocado Salsa:
2 x 175g (6oz) avocados
juice of ½ lemon (approx.
2 tbsp)
1 tbsp olive oil
½ tsp salt
10 grinds of black pepper
½ clove garlic, crushed
2 tomatoes, peeled and
roughly chopped
1 red pepper (bell pepper),
finely chopped
12 coriander seeds, crushed in
a mortar or with the end of
a rolling pin
4 rounded tbsp Greek yoghurt
or creamy fromage frais

For garnish:
half a red pepper
(bell pepper), seeded and
cut in julienne strips

1. Several hours in advance, prepare the Avocado Salsa. Put the peeled and stoned (pitted) avocado in the food processor or blender, together with the lemon juice, olive oil and seasonings, and process until smooth. Add the remaining ingredients and pulse only until blended. Taste and add more seasoning if desired.

2. Fold in the Greek yoghurt or creamy fromage frais. Cover with clingfilm (plastic wrap) and chill.

To grill the fish:
3. Lightly salt and pepper the washed and dried fish. Melt the butter in a grill (broiler) pan or roulade tin large enough to hold it in one layer. Before the butter begins to colour, lay the fish in it, then immediately turn it over so that it is coated on both sides.

4. Cook for 2 minutes under moderate heat, then turn the fish over. Dredge lightly with flour and grill very gently for a further 10 minutes, basting half way, until the fish flakes easily. (Don't overcook!)

To bake the fish:
5. Preheat the oven to 230°C (450°F/Gas 8). Oil and season the fish as before, then bake for 8–10 minutes, or until cooked through.

In either case:
6. Lift the fish out on to a warm serving plate and keep warm.

7. Add the almonds to the butter remaining in the dish and grill until golden, then stir in the lemon juice. Spoon some of the almond butter over each piece of fish and garnish with the red pepper.

8. Stir the Avocado Salsa, and serve either from a sauce boat or in an individual little dish for each guest.

Shoulder of Lamb with an Apricot & Pine Kernel Stuffing

Serves 8

Leftovers will keep 3 days in the refrigerator. Freeze cooked meat 2 months.

To make the stuffing:
1. Roughly chop the apricots. Melt the margarine in a small frying pan and cook the onion gently until softened and golden. Add the pine kernels and continue to sauté until golden.

2. Put all the other ingredients, except the egg, into a bowl. Mix in the onion, pine kernels and fat until well blended, then moisten with the beaten egg. The mixture should just cling together.

To stuff a pocketed shoulder:
3. Sprinkle the meat lightly with salt, then pack the stuffing in loosely and sew up into a neat shape.

To stuff and roll a shoulder:
4. Lay the meat, skin-side down, on a board, and cut out any lumps of fat. Spread the stuffing evenly over the meat, pushing it into any little folds. Roll up neatly and sew into a compact shape, or close with a skewer if this is possible.

5. Preheat the oven to 180°C (350°F/Gas 4).

6. Put a rack in a roasting tin and lay the meat on top. Sprinkle with the salt and pepper and dust lightly with the flour, then pour over the oil. Roast the meat for 2 hours, then sprinkle with the sugar or brush with the conserve. Increase the heat to 200°C (400°F/Gas 6), then cook for a further 20–30 minutes until a rich brown. Leave in a warm place (or in the oven turned down to 110°C (225°F/Gas ¼) for 15 minutes before carving.

To make the gravy:
7. Pour off all but 2 teaspoons of fat from the roasting tin. Mix the cornflour (cornstarch) smoothly with the water, then pour into the roasting tin and add the crumbled beef stock cube. Bring to the boil, stirring well, then season to taste with salt and pepper.

1.6–1.8kg (3½–4 lb) shoulder of lamb, boned and pocketed, or boned and left flat

For the stuffing:
125g (4oz/¾ cup) tenderized apricots
50g (2oz/¼ cup) margarine
1 medium onion, finely chopped
1 heaped tbsp pine kernels
grated rind of half lemon
½ tsp salt
10 grinds of black pepper
125g (4oz/2 cups) fresh breadcrumbs
½ tsp freeze-dried fines herbes (optional)
1 egg, beaten

For the coating:
1 tsp salt
10 grinds of black pepper
flour for dusting
2 tbsp oil
1 tbsp demerara sugar or apricot conserve

For the gravy:
2 tsp fat from the roasting tin
2 level tsp cornflour (cornstarch)
300 ml (10 floz/1¼ cups) cold water
1 crumbled beef stock (bouillon) cube
salt and pepper to taste

Tsimmes

Serves 6 as a main course, 8 as a side dish

Keeps 3 days in the refrigerator. Freeze 1 month.

900g (2 lb) slice of brisket
1.5kg (3¼ lb) carrots
4 slightly rounded tbsp
   golden (corn) syrup
¼ tsp white pepper
2 tsp salt
1 tbsp cornflour (corn-
   starch)
675g (1½ lb) potatoes

Variation
Pflaumen Tsimmes

225g (8oz/1½ cups)
   tenderized prunes and/or
225g (8oz/1½ cups)
   tenderized dried apricots.

*Add the fruit when the dish is
cooked for the second time.*

The archetypal Rosh Hashanah rib-sticking casserole dish – I serve it for lunch on the first day, followed by fresh fruit as a light relief.

1. Trim excess fat off the meat, leaving a thin edging, then cut the meat into 4cm (1½″) chunks.

2. Peel the carrots and cut into 1.25cm (½″) cubes.

3. Put the carrots and meat into a pan. Barely cover with hot water, then add 2 tbsp of the syrup, the pepper and ½ tsp of salt. Bring to the boil and simmer for 2 hours, either on top of the stove or in a slow oven, 150°C (300°F/Gas 2).

4. Skim, or, if possible, chill overnight so that most of the fat can be removed.

5. Lift out the meat and carrots and put into a large earthenware, enamel or enamelled-iron casserole.

6. Mix the cornflour (cornstarch) with enough water to make a smooth cream, then stir into the stock from the carrots and meat. Bring to the boil and pour over the carrots and meat.

7. Peel and cut the potatoes into 1.25cm (½″) cubes and arrange on top, adding extra boiling water if necessary so that they are just submerged. Sprinkle with the remaining 1½ tsp salt and 2 tablespoons of syrup.

8. Cover and bring to the boil on top of the stove, then transfer to a slow oven, 150°C (300°F/Gas 2), for 3½ hours. Uncover and taste, adding a little more syrup if necessary.

9. Allow to brown, uncovered, for a further 30 minutes, then serve. The potatoes should be slightly brown and the sauce slightly thickened.

M'rouzya Tajine (Moroccan Style Beef with Pears, Prunes & Honey)

Serves 8

Keeps 3 days in the refrigerator. Freeze 3 months

A Sephardi equivalent of Tsimmes. The dried pears are an inspiration! Serve this with very thin lokshen (linguine) to mop up the wonderful juices.

1. Preheat the oven to 160°C (325°F/Gas 3). Have ready a large casserole.

2. Heat the oil in a large frying or sauté pan. Add as many of the cubes of beef as will comfortably fit without crowding and brown on all sides. Transfer to a deep casserole. Repeat with the remaining meat, adding extra oil to the pan if needed.

3. Add the chopped onions to the same oil and cook until a rich golden brown. Add the spices, salt and pepper to the onions, and cook for 5 minutes more.

4. Add this mixture to the beef in the casserole, then pour in the hot stock mixed with the tomato purée (the meat should be barely submerged – adjust the amount of stock as required).

5. Bring to the boil on top of the stove, then cover and transfer to the oven. (If your casserole cannot be used to bring the liquid to the simmer on top of the stove, add an extra 30 minutes to the oven cooking time.)

6. Cook for 1½ hours, then add the dried fruit and honey. Re-cover and cook for a further 30 minutes or until the meat is meltingly tender. Check the casserole; if the sauce is too thick, add a little hot stock before serving.

7. Sprinkle the casserole with the sesame seeds which have been toasted by shaking in a small, heavy frying pan until golden. Garnish with the chopped fresh herb.

3 tbsp sunflower oil
1.8kg (4 lb) shoulder steak cut into 4cm (1½-inch) cubes
2 large onions, finely chopped
3 tsp paprika
3 tsp ground cinnamon
1 tsp ground ginger
2 tsp salt
20 grinds of black pepper
approx. 600 ml (1 pint/2½ cups) hot beef stock (using 1 cube)
1 rounded tbsp tomato purée (paste)

To add in last 30 minutes of cooking time:
250g (9oz) pack ready-to-eat pitted prunes
225g (8oz) dried pears (cut into bite-sized pieces)
1 rounded tbsp honey

For garnish:
2 rounded tbsp toasted sesame seeds
1 rounded tbsp of fresh coriander (cilantro) or parsley, coarsely chopped

Succulent Roast Chicken with a Lemon & Honey Glaze

Serves 6

Leftovers keep 3 days in the refrigerator. Freeze 3 months.

1 x 2–2.25kg (4½–5lb) chicken

1 fat garlic clove

olive oil for brushing the bird

salt and black pepper

300 ml (10 floz/1¼ cups) strong chicken stock, home-made or use 1 stock (bouillon) cube and 275 ml (10 floz/1¼ cups) water

For glazing the bird:

2 tbsp lemon juice

2 tbsp runny honey

For the gravy:

2 tsp cornflour (cornstarch)

2 tbsp water or white wine

To keep the breast meat juicy, the bird is cooked breast-side down and turned over to complete the browning only for the last 30 minutes.

When calculating the cooking time, allow an extra 15 minutes for the bird to 'settle' out of the oven before it is carved.

1. Preheat the oven to 200°C (400°F/Gas 6).

2. In a roasting tin that will just hold the bird comfortably, put a poultry cradle or grill (broiler) rack.

3. Make a shallow nick on each side of the bird where the leg joint meets the breast and insert half the peeled garlic clove in each. Brush the bird all over with olive oil and season with a sprinkling of sea salt and freshly ground black pepper.

4. Pour the hot stock into the roasting tin, then lay the bird upside down on the cradle (if it doesn't sit comfortably arrange it on its side). Roast it this way for 20 minutes per 450g (1 lb) plus 20 minutes – for a 2.25kg (5lb) bird the total cooking time will be 2 hours.

5. Baste the bird every 30 minutes with the stock. Then 30 minutes before the end of the cooking time, turn it over (a large wooden or metal spoon inserted in the cavity makes the job easier) and cook breast-side up for the remaining time.

6. Brush it with a mixture of half the lemon juice and honey, then repeat 15 minutes later.

7. Lift it on to a carving dish or board, then cover lightly with foil (to retain the heat).

8. Pour off any free fat and if some of the stock has dried up,

add enough boiling water to bring it back to the original 300 ml (10 floz/1¼ cups). Stir well to loosen any of the crispy bits on the bottom of the tin, then pour into a small pan and add the cornflour (cornstarch) mixed to a cream with the water or white wine. Bring to the boil and simmer for 3 minutes, but do be sure to taste it and correct the seasoning if necessary.

9. If the fat content of the meal has a high priority, discard the (alas delectable) skin – this will halve the calories of each serving

Chicken Breasts with Roasted Lemons

Serves: 6–8

Serve hot or cold. Keeps 3 days in the refrigerator.
Freeze 2 months. Do not reheat.

The golden breasts are bathed in a mouth-watering lemon sauce. The whole lemon can be eaten if the skin is tender; otherwise each guest can scoop out the delicious inside.

225g (8oz/1 cup) sugar
175 ml (6 floz/¾ cup) water
6–8 unwaxed lemons
6–8 boneless chicken
  breasts, skinned

1. Early on the day you plan to cook the dish, put the sugar and water into a pan just large enough to hold the lemons. Stir well over a gentle heat to dissolve the sugar.

2. Cut the lemons in half and trim off the knobbly bits from each end. Add to the sugar syrup and simmer uncovered for 10 minutes. Leave the lemons to go cold in the syrup.

3. Preheat the oven to 180°C(350°F/Gas 4).

4. Put the breasts in a roasting tin and pour the syrup over. Arrange the lemons round the chicken. Bake for 20–25 minutes or until cooked through.

5. Serve the chicken with the sauce, garnished with the lemons, and accompanied by a crisp green salad and bulgur wheat or rice.

A Casserole of Chicken in the Spanish Style

Serves 6–8

Keeps 2 days in the refrigerator. Freeze 3 months.

6–8 chicken breasts
  on the bone, skinned
1 heaped tbsp flour sea-
  soned with 2 tsp paprika
  and 15 grinds of black
  pepper
3 tbsp olive oil
sea salt
1 large onion, finely
  chopped
1 fat clove garlic, chopped
300 ml (10 floz/1¼ cups)
  passata (sieved tomatoes)
1 tbsp sun-dried tomato
  paste (preferably) or
  tomato purée
2 fat red peppers (bell peppers) halved, seeded and
  cut into 1.25cm
  (½-inch) squares
150 ml (5 floz/⅔ cup)
  chicken stock
150 ml (5 floz/⅔ cup) fruity
  red wine
2 tsp dark Muscovado sugar
15 grinds of black pepper
1 tsp salt
225g (8oz/2½ cups) button
  mushrooms, stalks
  trimmed level with caps
125g (4oz/1 cup) green
  olives, stoned (pitted)
  and roughly chopped
225g (8oz/1 cup)
  petits pois

A richly flavoured tomato sauce enlivens this casserole of chick-
en. The dish is particularly good-tempered and can be kept in a
low oven without spoiling for up to 30 minutes.

1. Preheat the oven to 180°C (350°F/Gas 4).

2. Thinly coat the chicken breasts with the seasoned flour, pat-
    ting off any excess. Heat the oil in a heavy frying pan, and
    brown the chicken pieces on all sides. Lift out and arrange
    breast-side up in a roasting tin. Sprinkle lightly with sea salt.

3. In the same oil, gently sauté the onion and garlic until soft
    and golden, then add the passata, tomato paste or purée, red
    pepper squares, stock, wine, sugar, pepper and 1 teaspoon of
    salt.

4. Simmer uncovered until the mixture is thick and juicy –
    about 5 minutes, then pour over and around the chicken
    breasts. They should be half-covered with the liquid. If not,
    add a little more stock.

5. Cover the roasting tin tightly with foil and bake the chicken
    for 45 minutes, basting once.

6. Uncover, then add the mushrooms, olives and petits pois,
    and baste again. Cover and cook for a further 15 minutes.

7. The dish can now be kept hot for up to 30 minutes in a very
    low oven, 120°C (250°F, Gas ½).

Ogen Summer Salad

Serves 6–8 or 10 with other salads

Use within 48 hours of preparation.

A glamourised version of Waldorf Salad, delicious with poached salmon or pickled brisket. It also looks stunning as a starter, served in tall slim glasses.

1. Several hours before the meal, stir together all the dressing ingredients, then put to one side.

2. Halve the melon, remove the seeds, then scoop out the flesh using a melon-ball cutter. Leave in a sieve to drain.

3. Cut the celery into 1cm ($\frac{3}{8}$ inch) cubes. Core and then quarter the apples and cut into cubes of the same size. Put in a bowl with the grapes and mix with the dressing.

4. Chill for several hours.

5. Half an hour before serving, stir in the melon. Garnish with the strawberries, sliced if large, and sprinkle with the nuts. Garnish with the sprigs of mint.

1 medium Ogen or other cantaloup-type melon
8 large, tender, inside stalks of celery
2 medium-sized, crisp, red-skinned eating apples
175g (6oz/1 cup) black seedless grapes, halved
225g (8oz/1½ cups) strawberries, hulled
25g (1oz/¼ cup) walnuts, coarsely chopped

For the dressing:
150 ml (5 floz/⅔ cup) mayonnaise
1 tsp each orange and lemon juice
1 tsp light Muscovado sugar
10 grinds of black pepper
1 tbsp finely chopped mint

For the garnish:
sprigs of mint

Ogen Summer Salad

More than any other dish, a salad dressing depends on the quality and freshness of the ingredients, of which one of the most important is salt. If you've always thought that salt is salt is salt, forget it – sea salt is the very latest 'designer' seasoning! What's more, if you go for the right kind, you will actually use less of it than ordinary cooking salt. This always comes complete with an anti-caking agent, which keeps the salt free-flowing but masks its saltiness with the result that you use more to compensate.

In Britain you can find sea salt crystals in the supermarket – two excellent brands are Maldon sea salt which is produced in Essex, and Baleine which comes from Aigues-Mortes in France's Camargue. These unrefined salt crystals not only taste superior to ordinary salt, but also contain trace elements such as magnesium and calcium that impart a subtle flavour.

For the real salt aficionado, however, nothing will do but 'sel gris' – the king of sea salt. Do remember that whether you use the coarse or fine sea salt, you will need less than usual. And only the coarse salt will do for a salt mill.

Fresh Pineapple, Mandarin & Black Grape Compôte

Serves 8

Keeps 2 days in the refrigerator. Do not freeze.

1 large fresh pineapple
4 large mandarins or
  oranges
75g (3oz/⅓ cup) caster
  (superfine) sugar
125 ml (4 floz/½ cup) water
75 ml (3 floz/⅓ cup) orange
  juice
juice of a lime
2 tsp cornflour (cornstarch)
juice of a large lemon
2 tbsp any orange-flavoured
  liqueur
225g (8oz/1½ cups) seedless
  black grapes

A mouth-watering combination of flavours: if at all possible use mandarins, which have a wonderful depth of flavour. The compôte is enhanced by serving with a sorbet of a complementary flavour, such as orange, lemon or pineapple.

1. Cut off the tufts from the pineapple. With a strong serrated knife (e.g. a bread knife), cut downwards to remove all the skin. Cut the flesh in half lengthways, then remove the woody core and cut the flesh into small pieces. Put in a large bowl.

2. Remove the skin from the mandarins or oranges, then slice or section and add to the pineapple.

3. In a small pan, dissolve the sugar in the water, stirring over moderate heat, then add the orange and lime juice.

4. Mix the cornflour (cornstarch) to a cream with the lemon juice. Stir into the hot liquid and bubble for 3 minutes to cook the starch, then stir in the liqueur. Pour over the pineapple pieces and mandarin sections, stirring gently.

5. Chill for several hours. No more than an hour before serving, stir in the grapes (this stops them becoming soggy).

Apple and Ginger Lekach

Serves 8 (photograph between pages 56 and 57)

Keeps 3 days in the refrigerator. Freeze 3 months.

A light, honeyed lekach is topped by a mouth-watering combination of stem ginger and baking apples. Serve at room temperature as a cake, warm as a pudding.

1. Preheat the oven to 190°C (375°F/Gas 5). Have ready a 22.5cm (9-inch) cake tin about 4–5cm (1½–2″) deep.

2. Melt the fat in a pan, then use a little to grease the tin.

To make the topping:
3. Peel, core and slice the apples finely (most easily done in the food processor).

4. Add the sugar and the tablespoon of honey to the melted fat and cook, stirring, until a rich golden brown. Mix thoroughly with the apples and ginger, then place in an even layer in the tin.

To make the sponge:
5. Put the margarine, sugar, liquid honey and egg into a bowl or food processor. Beat or process until smooth. Finally stir in the flour, sifted alternately with the spices and the bicarbonate of soda dissolved in the water. The batter will be thin.

6. Pour over the apples and bake for 40 minutes or until firm to the touch. Leave 5 minutes, then turn out and serve plain or with Greek yoghurt or ice-cream.

7. To reheat, put the pudding on a heatproof serving plate and cover with the cake tin. Heat at 190°C (375°F/Gas 5) for 15 minutes or until warm to the touch. To reheat in the microwave, cook uncovered at 80 per cent power for 2 minutes.

For the apple topping:
3 large Bramley baking apples (unpeeled weight 700 g/1½ lb)
50g (2oz/¼ cup) dark Muscovado sugar
1 rounded tbsp honey
50g (2oz/¼ cup) butter or margarine
3 pieces stem ginger, cut in little cubes

For the ginger sponge:
125g (4oz/½ cup) soft margarine
125g (4oz/½ cup) light Muscovado sugar
175g (6oz/½ cup) liquid honey
1 egg
225g (8oz/2 cups) plain (all-purpose) flour
2 level tsp ground ginger
½ tsp mixed sweet spice or cinnamon
½ tsp bicarbonate soda (cooking soda)
125 ml (4 floz/½ cup) warm water

Miniature Lekach (variation)

Makes 24

Keep 2 weeks at room temperature in an airtight container. Freeze 3 months.

These little cakes are ideal for smaller households.

1. Omit the apple topping.

2. Put 1 level tbsp of the ginger sponge mixture in each of 24 paper cases.

3. Bake at 190°C (375°/Gas 5) for 20 minutes until a rich brown and spongy to gentle touch.

Filo Pastry Tarte with a Caramelized Apple Filling

Serves 6–8

The cooked tarte may be refrigerated overnight and then briefly reheated. Freeze 1 month.

1 x 400g (14oz) pack filo
  (phyllo) pastry
75g (3oz/¾ stick)
  unsalted butter, melted

For preparing the flan dish:
1 tsp melted butter
1 tbsp sugar

For the filling:
1.3kg (3lb) crisp flavourful
  eating apples
50g (2oz/¼ cup)
  unsalted butter
125g (4oz/½ cup)
  light Muscovado sugar
1 tbsp lemon juice
125g (4oz) marzipan,
  coarsely grated (optional)

The ready-made filo (phyllo) pastry, which in this version stands in for the 'croustade' of south-west France, gives this easily made tarte a wonderfully light texture.

1. Preheat the oven to 220°C (425°F/Gas 7).

2. For the filling: peel the apples, then core and cut each into 12 wedges.

3. In a very large frying pan over a medium heat, melt the butter for the filling, then stir in the sugar and continue to heat until an even mixture. Add the apples to the pan (don't worry if they seem too packed as they will shrink when some of the juice comes out of them.) Toss them in the pan until each piece of apple is golden brown in colour, then sprinkle with the lemon juice. Lift out the apples with a slotted spoon.

4. Boil down any remaining liquid until thick and syrupy (there may be 3–4 tbsp liquid remaining, depending on the variety of apple used). Spoon over the apples and allow to cool.

5. Grease the inside of a round 22.5–25cm (9–10-inch) ceramic flan dish with the butter and dust with the tablespoon of sugar.

6. Take eight sheets of filo from the pack and cut into 30cm (12-inch) squares. Lay five of these squares on top of each other (patch if necessary) in the dish, brushing each in turn with the melted butter. Trim level with the edge, forming a lower 'crust'.

7. Scatter the pastry with grated marzipan (if used) and arrange the apples in an even layer on top.

8. Now cut the remaining three sheets of filo (and any trimmings) into roughly 15cm (6-inch) triangles. Brush lightly with butter, then crumple up in the hand like a chiffon scarf to make small mounds. Arrange these on top of the apple, completely covering them. Sprinkle with any remaining melted butter and then with the caster sugar.

9. Bake for 20–25 minutes until the top is golden and the sugar has caramelized, producing a wonderful glaze.

10. Serve warm from the dish. May be reheated either in the oven or (carefully) under the grill (broiler), sprinkled with a little extra caster sugar.

For the topping:
50g (2oz/¼ cup) caster (superfine) sugar

Filo Pastry Tarte with a Caramelized Apple Filling

In south-west France, they make a tarte of paper-thin pastry called, according to the district, 'le pastis', 'la croustarde' or 'la tourtière'. You and I would call this stretched pastry 'filo' as it is made exactly the same way as the Austrian 'Strudelteig'.

It is thought to have come to France from Spain – and to be closely related to the B'stilla pastry of the Moors who ruled that country for so many centuries. It is a skill handed down from mother to daughter in this part of France. Without such an apprenticeship, it's simpler to buy a pack of filo from the supermarket!

Whatever you call it, it make marvellous featherlight tartes!

Traditional Anglo-Jewish Lekach

Makes one 30 x 2 x 5cm (12 x 9 x 2″) cake, which cuts into 48 pieces, each 4cm (1?1/2″) square

Keeps 2 weeks at room temperature, wrapped in foil in an airtight container.
Freeze 1 month (spicing fades if frozen longer).

450g (1 lb/1⅓ cups) honey
300 ml (10 floz/1¼ cups) cold
  water
200g (7oz/1 cup) granulated
  sugar
225 ml (8 floz/1 cup) flavourless oil (e.g. sunflower)
3 eggs
450g (1 lb/4 cups)
  self-raising flour
  (or use plain (all-purpose)
  flour with 4 level tsp
  baking powder)
1 level tsp each of ground ginger, cinnamon and mixed
  sweet spice
1 level tsp baking powder
1 level tsp bicarbonate of soda
  (baking soda)
50 ml (2 floz) plus 2 tsp
  Kiddush (port-type) red wine

This is one of those recipes of unknown origin, that is passed from hand to hand because it is so superb – light yet moist and so easy to make. Unlike other lekach, it does not need to mature before use, but may be served as soon as it is cold.

1. Preheat the oven to 200°C (400°F/Gas 6).

2. Lightly brush with oil a baking tin measuring 30 x 22.5 x 5cm (12 x 9 x 2″) and line the base and short sides with a piece of silicone paper.

3. Heat the honey, water, sugar and oil over gentle heat, stirring until the mixture is smooth and the sugar has dissolved.

4. In a large bowl, whisk the eggs together until creamy and frothy, then gradually add the honey mixture, mixing with a wooden spoon or balloon whisk all the time.

5. Finally, gradually stir in all the dry ingredients which have been sifted together, and the bicarbonate of soda dissolved in the wine. Make sure the mixture is smooth and even in colour.

6. Pour into the tin and then put in the oven.

7. Immediately turn the heat down to 150°C (300°F/Gas 2) and bake for 1¼–1½ hours, or until firm to the touch and a rich brown. Leave the cake (still in the tin) on a cooling rack.

8. When it is cool to the touch, turn the tin over on to the cooling rack and ease the cake out, then immediately turn it right side up on to another cooling rack. Alternatively, it can be left in the tin and pieces cut as required. Wrap in foil when quite cold.

Traditional Anglo-Jewish Lekach

Honey is a familiar ingredient in Jewish cookery – not surprisingly considering it's the oldest sweetener known to man – dating back to the first human settlements when early peoples raided the honey-bee colonies. Jewish dishes still sweetened with honey include dried fruit compôte, lekach and tsimmes – and does anybody still make that wonderful honey-based drink, mead?

Marillen or Schwetzken Kuchen (Apricot or Plum Gateau)

Serves 8–12 (photograph between pages 56 and 57)

Serve the same day if possible. Leftovers keep 2 days in the refrigerator.
Freeze leftovers 1 month.

This is an Anglo-Jewish version of the marvellous Austro-Hungarian cake (the base is really a featherlight Victoria sponge), but the topping for the plum version should use the wonderful schwetzken plums (or other freestone plums). For best results, use a wide oven-to-table flan dish, and be generous with the fruit.

1. Preheat the oven to 180°C (350°F/Gas 4). Lightly oil the inside of a 25cm (10-inch) oven-to-table flan dish.

2. Put all the sponge ingredients into a mixing bowl and beat with a wooden spoon or electric mixer until smooth and creamy – 2–3 minutes. If using a food processor, put all the ingredients into the bowl and process for 10 seconds. Take off the cover and scrape down the sides of the bowl with a rubber spatula. Replace the cover, then process for a further 5 seconds.

3. Turn the cake batter into the prepared flan dish and smooth level. Cover completely with the apricots or plums, flesh-side up. Sprinkle with half the mixed sugar and cinnamon.

4. Bake the cake for 40 minutes or until it is golden brown and firm to the touch, and a skewer comes out clean from the centre. Sprinkle with the remaining sugar and cinnamon.

5. Serve at room temperature, either plain or with fromage frais or ice-cream.

For the sponge:
125g (4oz/½ cup) soft margarine
125g (4oz/½ cup) caster (superfine) sugar
125g (4oz/1 cup) self-raising flour (or plain (all-purpose) flour with 1 level tsp baking powder)
2 large eggs
grated rind of ½ lemon

For the topping:
900g (2 lb) ripe apricots or plums, halved and stoned (pitted)
75g (3oz/⅓ cup) granulated sugar mixed with 1 tsp cinnamon

Fluffy Chocolate Fingers

Makes about 30 fingers

Keeps 1 week in an airtight container. Freeze 6 months.

2 eggs
200g (7oz/1 cup) golden
    caster (superfine) sugar
150g (5oz/⅔ cup) soft mar-
    garine
1 tsp vanilla extract
3 tbsp boiling water
75g (3oz/¾ cup) sponge self-
    raising flour (or plain
    (all-purpose) flour with ½
    level tsp baking powder)
4 level tbsp cocoa

*For sprinkling on the cooked
fingers:*
2 tbsp caster (superfine)
    sugar

Quickly made, ultra-light sweet treats for New Year tea parties.

1. Preheat the oven to 180°C (350°F/Gas 4). Grease an 18–20cm (7–8″) square tin which is at least 2.5cm (1″) deep.

2. In a food processor, process the eggs and sugar for 2 minutes. Divide the margarine into 4 or 5 lumps and drop on top, then pulse 2 or 3 times until it disappears.

3. Add the vanilla extract and the boiling water and process until smooth – about 2 seconds. Add the flour and cocoa and pulse until they too disappear.

4. Clean down the sides of the bowl with a rubber spatula.

5. Turn into the prepared container and bake for 30 minutes, or until the top springs back when gently pressed.

6. Allow to cool for 5 minutes on a cooling tray. After 10 minutes, sprinkle lightly with caster sugar.

7. Divide into fingers. Store in an airtight container when quite cold.

Almond Butter Crisps

Makes 48

Keeps 1 week in an airtight container. Freeze 6 months.

If you have time to make just one kind of biscuit, let it be this buttery, crunchy, crinkle-topped one!

1. Preheat the oven to 180°C (350°F/Gas 4).

2. Work the sugar into the butter using a wooden spoon, mixer or food processor. When the sugar has been absorbed, add the vanilla extract and the flour sifted with the bicarbonate of soda.

3. Roll into balls the size of a small walnut, approx. 2.5cm (1 inch) in diameter. Arrange on ungreased baking trays, leaving room for the biscuits to flatten and spread.

4. Decorate the tops with the almond nibs.

5. Bake for 15 minutes or until golden. Remove from the oven and allow to set for 5 minutes, then transfer to a cooling tray.

175g (6oz/¾ cup) caster (superfine) sugar
200g (7oz/1 cup) butter
1 tsp vanilla extract
225g (8oz/2 cups) self-raising flour (or plain (all-purpose) flour with 2 level tsp baking powder)
1 level tsp bicarbonate of soda (baking soda)
50g (2oz/½ cup) almond nibs or flaked (slivered) almonds

Almond Butter Crisps

Everyone loves a home-made biscuit, and the Almond Butter Crisps are very special. With their crinkled top, they look as though they've taken hours to shape – in fact you simply roll the biscuit mixture into little balls and let the oven do the rest. Another plus: if you can keep the family away from the biscuit tin for 2 or 3 days, the flavour will actually have improved!

What can be so special about a biscuit that contains only run-of-the-mill ingredients such as butter, sugar and flour? There's one thing in particular that sets these delectable nibbles apart – the vanilla flavouring.

Supermarkets now sell little bottles of 'vanilla extract', far superior but dearer than the 'vanilla flavouring' they also carry. But there are two forms of vanilla that are even better: 'Bourbon Vanilla Sugar' and 'Madagascar Bourbon Vanilla Extract', both now available in speciality food shops and some supermarkets. And if you do much baking, it's worth burying a few vanilla pods (beans) in your caster (superfine) sugar.

Two Challot for Rosh Hashanah

Makes 2 medium round loaves.

Keeps 3–4 days at room temperature in a bread container. Freeze baked 3 months.

1 sachet easy blend yeast
675g (1½ lb/6 cups) white
  strong (bread) flour
50g (2oz /¼ cup) sugar or 2
  rounded tbsp honey
1½ tsp salt
2 large eggs
325 ml (11 floz/1⅓ cups)
  warm water
5 tbsp sunflower (canola) or
  other flavourless oil

For the glaze:
1 egg yolk
2 tsp water
good pinch of salt
poppy seeds or sesame seeds

A labour of love, but amply repaid by the pleasure these two loaves bring to both the baker and the 'consumer'. They are most easily made with easy-blend yeast and the dough hook of an electric mixer.

1. Mix the yeast thoroughly with the flour and salt, then add the eggs, water, oil and honey or sugar to the bowl.

2. Now mix at low speed until a sticky ball begins to form. Then turn to medium speed and knead for 4 or 5 minutes until the dough is slapping against the edge of the bowl, leaving it clean as it goes round. If it looks sticky, work in a further 1 or 2 tablespoons of flour.

3. Tip the dough on to a floured board and knead with the hands for a further minute, until it is tight and springy with a silky feel.

4. Grease a large bowl with oil and turn the dough into it to coat it (this stops the surface drying out). Cover with clingfilm (plastic wrap) and leave to rise in the refrigerator. If it rises before you have time to deal with it (it takes from 9 to 12, hours but can be left for up to 24 hours), punch it down and leave it to rise again.

5. To shape the loaves: take the risen dough from the refrigerator and leave it to come to room temperature in the kitchen – about 1 hour. (Alternatively, put it on the Defrost cycle in a microwave oven for 2 minutes until warm to the touch.)

6. Divide the dough into 2 pieces and work on each half (each piece makes 1 loaf) as follows: knead the dough by hand or machine to break down any large bubbles of gas, then leave for 5 minutes to tighten up under a cloth.

7. Roll the dough into a long 'snake' about 45cm (18″) long and 4cm (1½″) in diameter. Take the left-hand end of the 'snake' and start coiling it round on itself, making a spiral, so that when all the dough has been wound round, the end you started with will

be on top and the right-hand end can be tucked underneath.
Repeat with the second piece of dough.

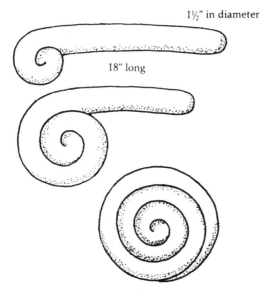

1½" in diameter

18" long

8. Mix together the yolk, water and salt for the glaze, then paint
    the mixture all over the loaves and scatter with the seeds.

9. To prove the loaves: arrange the loaves on 1 large or 2 smaller
    lightly greased baking trays. Slip the trays into a large plastic bag
    and leave in the kitchen until the loaves have almost doubled in
    size, feel light and spongy to the touch and spring back immedi-
    ately when lightly pressed with a finger. This takes 30–40 min-
    utes.

10. Preheat the oven to 220°C (425°F/Gas 7).

11. Bake the bread for 25 minutes, then turn the oven down to
    200°C (400°F/Gas 6) for a further 10–15 minutes, or until the
    bread is a rich brown.

12. Lift the loaves off the tray and tap the bottom. If the bread
    sounds hollow, take them out, otherwise, leave them in the oven
    for another 5 minutes and tap the bottom again.

13. When cooked, remove to a cooling tray.

Yom Kippur
The Day of Atonement
BEFORE AND AFTER THE FAST

For the meals to be served before and after the Fast of Yom Kippur, most families follow their own 'minhag' (custom) which is usually based on years of experience and family tradition.

Before the Fast

According to the best dietetic advice, it's easier to fast on two light meals rather than on one heavy one which may make you hungrier later on and less able to concentrate on the Service. In addition to cooked vegetables, it's best to eat small amounts of protein, such as fish or chicken, in order to maintain stable blood-sugar levels. Hot foods are more settling to the system and will sustain you through the Fast better than raw and cold foods. Avoid spices, which could create a thirst, then finish the meal with a piece of fresh fruit and a glass of lemon tea.

The custom in Holland is quite different – there is a two-course main meal at lunchtime, followed by a light meal eaten just before leaving for the synagogue.

After the Fast

When the husband and wife come from different ethnic back-grounds – such as Sephardi and Ashkenazi – their family customs will be quite different! To solve this dilemma, one woman I know serves the kugelhopf cake of her Viennese childhood, but accom-panies it with 'nanna' (green tea and spearmint) mixed with a spoonful of whisked egg and sugar for the sake of her Moroccan-born husband. In another household, everybody starts the Fast on chicken and rice, but for breaking the Fast, the wife serves a dairy and fish meal, Ashkenazi-style, while her Israeli/Turkish husband insists on chicken soup and bread soaked in olive oil!

I would hazard a guess, however, that in most Anglo-Jewish households, the 'minhag' goes something like this: a glass of Kiddush wine, which on this particular occasion during the year tastes like nectar, followed by copious cups of tea or coffee with lightly buttered kuchen (bun loaf). Then it's time for something tasty, usually pickled or smoked fish to tickle the taste-buds after a day of abstinence, then perhaps a low-fat milk-based soup and a maincourse of fish – for convenience usually chopped and fried (see p. 8) or Gefilte Fish Provençal (p. 12). Finally there is a light dessert for those with enough stamina to stay the course.

For breaking the Fast therefore, I have four suggestions, all of which can be made up to two days in advance and will actually improve in flavour during this time.

The Herring Salad, German Style, combines fat matjes (schmaltz) herring slices with crunchy apples and vegetables in a gently flavoured sour cream sauce. The Spicy Fish Salad is milder, being based on white fish flaked in a vinaigrette dressing which is enlivened with chilli powder and herbs. Chopped walnuts add a welcome crunch, but can be omitted if preferred. A soup based on fresh celery is eminently digestible, while for those who prefer a mildly flavoured pâté, one based on mushrooms puréed with hard-boiled eggs will make a satisfying alternative.

Cream of Celery Soup de luxe

Serves 6–8

Keeps 2 days in the refrigerator. Freeze 2 months.

1 fat head of celery,
   including 'crown'
   and leaves
25g (1oz/2 tbsp) butter
1 large (200 g/7oz) onion,
   finely chopped
1 litre (1¾ pints/4½ cups)
   good vegetable stock
2 bay leaves
1 tsp salt
15 grinds of black pepper
good pinch of white pepper
2 level tbsp cornflour
   (cornstarch)
600 ml (1 pint/2½ cups)
   milk
1 tsp freeze-dried fines
   herbes
¼ tsp ground nutmeg
snipped chives for garnish

Cream Of Celery Soup

The true flavour of the celery (especially the blanched variety) is in the base, to which the stalks are attached, so after removing the discoloured 5 mm (?1/4 inch) which has been in the soil, use all the remainder in the soup. Some varieties of celery are stringless, others may need to be sieved as well as puréed to remove the strings.

A richly-flavoured but soothing soup to include in an after-the-Fast meal.

1. Cut off and discard 5 mm (¼ inch) from the root end of the celery.

2. Melt the butter gently in a large soup pan and add the chopped onion. Cover and simmer for 5 minutes.

3. Meanwhile, slice the celery root, stalks and leaves as thinly as possible, most easily in a food processor. Add to the onion, stir well, then add the stock, together with the bay leaves, salt and pepper. Bring to the boil, cover and simmer very gently for 30 minutes.

4. Remove the bay leaves. Blend or liquidize the mixture, most easily with an immersion blender. Do this thoroughly to ensure no celery strings remain.

5. Put the cornflour (cornstarch) in a bowl and add the milk gradually, then add to the celery purée, together with the fines herbes and nutmeg. Bring slowly to the boil, then simmer very gently, stirring until it starts to bubble and thicken.

6. Simmer for 5 minutes, then allow to stand for several hours or overnight to develop the flavour. Reheat to simmering point before serving, garnished with the snipped chives.

Herring Salad, German Style

Serves 8. When used as part of a buffet, serves 10 (photograph between pages 56 and 57)

Keeps 3 days in the refrigerator.

A mildly flavoured piquant salad, ideal to coax the taste-buds to life after a day of abstinence!

1. Drain the herrings thoroughly on paper towels, then cut into 1cm ($\frac{1}{2}$″) slices.

2. Peel and core the apple, then cut downwards into 5-mm ($\frac{1}{4}$″) thick segments and cut each segment in turn into 1cm ($\frac{1}{2}$″) wide pieces.

3. Cut both the cucumber and the beetroot into tiny dice.

4. Spoon the soured cream into a large bowl, then stir in the sugar and vinegar. Finally, stir in all the prepared ingredients.

5. Cover and chill for several hours.

6. To serve as a starter, arrange on a bed of crisp shredded lettuce or, more decoratively, in a Paris goblet – or other wine glass with a rounded bowl. Serve chilled.

1 x 500g pack (400 g/14oz drained weight) Matjes (schmaltz) herrings
1 large (225 g/8oz) Bramley (cooking) apple
2 small 10–13cm (4–5-inch) pickled cucumbers
2 plain boiled beetroots (beets)
1 x 300 ml (10 floz/1¼ cup) carton soured cream
2 tsp caster (superfine) sugar
2 tsp wine vinegar or cider vinegar

Herring Salad

'It is the food of the poor, but it is also the delicacy of the rich . . . [and] it could be claimed that each Jew eats one a day.' The words are those of the French chef, Edouard de Pomiane, writing about the humble salt herring shortly after the First World War. And although Pomiane was writing about Poland, it could surely apply to the whole of Eastern Europe and beyond, particularly in the 18th and 19th centuries. For the aristocracy of Czarist Russia, the salt herring in its many manifestations was an essential part of the 'zakuski' table, whose tasty titbits were considered the ideal partners for a glass or three of vodka.

For the poor Jews of the Pale of Settlement, the herring was a cheap and nourishing form of protein – give menfolk a couple of herrings a day and expensive meat could be kept for a Shabbat treat.

Salt herrings in the barrel came from as far afield as Scotland (they were often bartered for Dutch coffee and tea when foreign trawlers put in to remote Highland lochs), but most came from Holland and Germany. As in those days, the most delicious are undoubtedly the schmaltz (matjes) herrings, so-called because of their soft succulent flesh which is found only in the first young herrings caught between May and July when the roes are immature and all the goodness is still in the fish itself.

The Dutch call these 'maatjes haring' (young herring) or 'groene (green) haring' and their fishermen are said to have invented the distinctive mild cure. An earlier generation could buy only whole schmaltz herrings, which needed to be filleted and soaked before use. Then someone had the idea of selling them as fillets, which were much more convenient but had a very short 'shelf' life. Now the latest – and most convenient pack – will keep unopened for up to three months in the refrigerator. These herrings are packed in a little vegetable oil and can be used straight from the pack.

Spicy Fish Salad

Serves 8–10 as part of a buffet, 6 as a starter

Keeps 3 days in the refrigerator. Do not freeze.

900g (2 lb) cod
  or haddock fillets
1 tsp sugar
pinch of white pepper
1½ tsp salt

For the dressing:
2 tbsp chopped parsley
2 medium cloves of garlic,
  crushed
6 tbsp sunflower (canola) oil
2 tbsp walnut
  or hazelnut oil
1 tbsp fresh lemon juice
4 tbsp white wine vinegar or
  cider vinegar
1 tsp mild chilli powder
15 grinds of black pepper
½ tsp salt
2 rounded tbsp fromage frais
  or Greek yoghurt
125g (4oz/1 cup) walnuts,
  coarsely chopped

'Tasty' is the best way to describe this fish salad with a French accent. Serve in a pottery bowl lined with lettuce leaves or spoon into halves of avocado which have been brushed with lemon juice to prevent discoloration.

1. Place the fish in a saucepan with barely enough water to cover and add the sugar, pepper and salt. Poach very gently for 20 minutes, covered on top of the stove, or for 6 minutes on 100 per cent power in a microwave.

2. Cool for 5 minutes, then lift the fish out with a slotted spoon. Place in a bowl and flake roughly with a fork.

3. In a large bowl, whisk together all the dressing ingredients except the walnuts. Then fold these in and spoon the dressing on top of the fish. Toss gently together, then chill.

4. Garnish with a pinch of paprika before serving.

Mushroom Pâté

Serves 6 as a starter, 8–12 as a spread

Keeps 2 days in the refrigerator. Do not freeze.

This pâté is also delicious spread on buttered challah, to accompany the cup of tea or coffee at the conclusion of the Fast.

1. Sauté the onions and the garlic in the hot oil and butter until soft and golden.

2. Add the mushrooms, sprinkle with the seasonings and continue to cook until brown and slightly caramelized.

3. Put the contents of the frying pan and their juices in a food processor with the eggs and parsley and process until a thick paste (there should be a little texture left).

4. Turn into a dish and chill. Serve garnished with the chopped parsley.

2 medium onions,
   thinly sliced
2 large cloves of garlic,
   finely chopped
3 tbsp sunflower (canola)
   or olive oil
2 tbsp butter
450g (1 lb) brown-cap
   mushrooms, coarsely
   chopped
tsp ground nutmeg or mace
1 tsp sea salt
15 grinds of black pepper
6 hard-boiled eggs, shelled
   and quartered
several sprigs of parsley

For the garnish:
2 tsp chopped parsley

Sukkot/Simchat Torah
Tabernacles/The Rejoicing of the Law

Sukkot is undoubtedly one of the happier Festivals of the year. It's the colours and perfumes associated with its celebration that come to mind – the shiny purple aubergines and the spiky white chrysanthemums, the muscatel grapes and the fragrant melons, and above all, the once-a-year sight and smell of the fruit-and-vegetable-decorated Sukkah.

Sukkot is a celebration of the good things of life – food and wine and flowers, and the companionship of our family and friends. It is the third of the Pilgrim Festivals, an expression of thanks for the harvest and its bounty. However, it is mainly a reminder of the 40 years the Children of Israel wandered in the wilderness between Egypt and the Promised Land, living in temporary shelters, an event we recall every year by making our own Sukkah or helping to build and decorate the ones at our synagogues.

Immediately after the end of the Yom Kippur Fast, it is the custom for the men in the congregation to make a symbolic start to the construction of the Sukkah. It is essentially a temporary structure – open to the sky, but decorated with sweet-smelling and colourful harvest fruit and flowers. Many people who have built a Sukkah at home eat all their meals in it for the whole seven days; others invite friends to join them there for a glass of wine and a slice of delicious cake such as the Apfelkuchen Squares or the Dried Fruit Strudel with a Flaky Cream Cheese Pastry.

This is the Festival of plenty, so 'stuffed' fruit and vegetables are on every menu. Dishes such as Aubergines in Apricot Sauce, Holishkes and Gevikelte Kraut (stuffed cabbage), Stuffed Vine Leaves and Fresh Peach and Macaroon Strudel are a joy to make as well as a pleasure to eat. I have also included innovative dishes such as the Blitze Torte with its mouth-watering filling of caramelized pineapple and cream, and the Crystallized Ginger Slice which is layered with fresh mango. A luscious râgout of aubergine, peppers and tomato is perfect for those who want a lighter dish, and for a light *Succoth* supper, nothing could be more mouth-watering than a melon soup marbled with swirls of fresh raspberry purée.

Not only do we commemorate the harvest in the Succah itself, but in the synagogue there is the beautiful ceremony of passing from hand to hand the 'lulav' – a sheaf of willow, palm and myrtle branches, and delighting in the perfume of that wonderful citrus fruit, the etrog (citron). A rabbi and his wife who every year make a superb marmalade from this fruit, gave me their recipe, which I am thrilled to pass on.

One writer has suggested that Sukkot is really the Festival of the ephemeral: the temporary Sukkah which lasts but a week, the fruit and vegetables which have such a brief moment of ripe perfection, the autumn sun which soon gives way to the chill of winter, and the wonderful food which we serve to our guests when the pastry is still crisp, the cakes still fresh – a reminder that life is to be lived and celebrated in the here and now.

The very end of the month of Festivals is Simchat Torah, the Rejoicing of the Law, when all the Scrolls of the Law are taken out of the Ark and paraded round the synagogue no less than seven times, giving every one the chance to sing and dance, as the last and first portions of the Five Books of Moses are read by the two members of the Congregation who are to be specially honoured.

So rejoice!

Gevikilte Kraut

Serves 6 as a starter, 4 as a main course

Keeps 3 days in the refrigerator. Freeze leftovers 3 months.

1 firm head of white
   cabbage

For the stuffing:
450g (1 lb) minced
   (ground) raw steak
2 level tbsp medium
   matzah meal
1 level tsp salt
pinch of white pepper
1 egg, beaten
½ onion, grated

For the sauce:
2 tbsp wine vinegar or
   cider vinegar
2 generous tbsp golden
   (corn) syrup
1 bay leaf
5 peppercorns
1 level tsp salt
300ml (10 floz/1¼ cups)
   beef stock or thin gravy

This has a delicious sweet-and-sour meat sauce and actually tastes better if it can be left in the refrigerator for 2 days before it is served, either hot or cold.

1. The day before cooking , freeze the cabbage for 12 hours, then defrost overnight at room temperature, or for 30 minutes on 'defrost' in a microwave. The leaves will then peel off like a dream if detached from the stalk end using a small, sharp knife.

2. Preheat the oven to 180°C (350°F/Gas 4).

3. Mix all the stuffing ingredients together.

4. Detach 12 large leaves from the defrosted cabbage. Stuff each leaf, one at a time, by placing a rounded tablespoonful of the stuffing in the centre, turning in the sides and rolling up into a bundle. Lift each bundle and give a gentle squeeze with the palm of the hand to seal it.

5. Lay the bundles side by side in a shallow-lidded or foil-covered casserole.

6. Mix all the sauce ingredients together and spoon them over the cabbage bundles, adding extra stock if necessary so that they are barely covered, and cover with the lid or foil.

7. Put in the oven for 30 minutes. The sauce will then be simmering. Turn the oven down to 150°C (300°F/Gas 2) and cook for a further 2 hours.

8. Fifteen minutes before the end of the cooking time, uncover and turn the heat up to 180°C (350°F/Gas 4) to brown the tops of the cabbage bundles and thicken the sauce.

Holishkes (Meat-stuffed cabbage leaves braised in a sweet and sour tomato sauce)

Serves 6 as a starter, 4 as a main course

The holishkes will taste even better if they can be kept in the refrigerator for up to 2 days before using. Freeze leftovers for up to 3 months.

1. Freeze and defrost the cabbage as for the Gevikilte Kraut, then detach at least 12 leaves.

2. Cook the onion in the oil or fat until golden and tender, then add the rice and cook for 3 minutes until opaque.

3. Add the stock and cook gently until absorbed, then stir into the meat, together with the seasonings.

4. Lay at least 12 cabbage leaves on a board. Put 1 tablespoon of filling on each and fold in the edges to enclose the filling. Roll up to make bundles, then squeeze gently between the palms to seal.

5. Pack closely in a large casserole.

6. Preheat the oven to 150° (300°F/Gas 2).

7. Mix the sauce ingredients together with the water and pour over the cabbage bundles.

8. Cover the casserole and cook the holishkes for 2½ hours. Then uncover, baste well and turn up the oven to 180°C (350°F/Gas 4) for a further 20–30 minutes to brown the holishkes and thicken the sauce.

1 firm head of white cabbage
1 onion, peeled and finely chopped
2 tbsp chicken-flavoured fat, sunflower (canola) oil or margarine
4 tbsp long-grain rice
125 ml (4 floz/½ cup) chicken stock
450g (1 lb) lean minced (ground) beef
1 tsp salt
10 grinds of black pepper

For the sauce:
150g (5oz/⅔ cup) tomato purée
½ tsp salt
black pepper
4 tbsp light Muscovado sugar
juice of 1 lemon
300 ml (10 floz/1¼ cups) water

Gevikilte Kraut

For the Festival of Sukkot, stuffed vegetables are high on the menu for both Ashkenazi and Sephardi households – and they come with a bewildering array of names and ingredients. Cabbage stuffed with minced meat is known in Ashkenazi families as either holishkes, holopches, praakes or galuptzi.

Sephardi Jews – particularly those who once lived in the former Ottoman Empire – call a similar dish, usually made with lamb instead of beef, dolmas col or yaprakis de kol. Cooks from the Middle East talk about sarmas or mishi malfouf.

Although the most familiar dish in the Anglo-Jewish cuisine is the one using cabbage, there is an infinite variety of other vegetables that can be used –aubergines (eggplant), green peppers, courgettes (zucchini), tomatoes, leeks, vine leaves, even carrots (though you need a special 'excavator' a bit like an apple corer for that).

Cabbage seems to have been the favoured Eastern European vegetable, probably because it was cheap and in season at Sukkot. The meat is 'extended' with matzah meal rather than rice as in Sephardi versions.

My Gevikilte kraut dish comes from Moscow, and uses a sweet-and-sour sauce based on beef stock or gravy.

Tourte à la Courge (Savoury Squash Tourte)

Serves 8

Keeps 2 days in the refrigerator. Freeze 1 month. Reheats well.

For the pastry:
225g (8oz/2 cups) plain (all-purpose) white or fine brown flour
½ tsp salt
2 tsp icing (powdered) sugar
1 tsp freeze-dried herbes de Provence
1 rounded tbsp chopped parsley
1 tsp dry mustard
150g (5oz/1⅓ cups) butter or block margarine
1 egg, beaten with 1 tsp wine vinegar or cider vinegar and 1 tbsp cold water

For the filling:
675–900g (1½–2 lb) orange or yellow-fleshed squash, e.g. acorn
or butternut
3 tbsp olive oil
1 large salad (mild) onion, peeled and finely sliced
4 whole eggs + 1 egg yolk
225 ml (8 floz/1 cup) whipping cream
15 grinds of black pepper
1 tsp salt
¼ tsp ground nutmeg
3 tsp cornflour (cornstarch)
25g (1oz/2 tbsp) finely grated Parmesan or Cheddar cheese

This makes a tasty, satisfying lunch or supper dish, accompanied by a crisp green or tomato salad.

1. To make the pastry in a food processor, put the dry ingredients, herbs and the well-chilled fat (cut into 2.5cm/1-inch chunks) into the bowl. Mix the egg, water and vinegar, then turn on the machine and pour this liquid down the feed tube, pulsing only until the mixture looks like a very moist crumble. Then tip it into a bowl and gather together into a dough.

3. Turn the pastry on to a board or counter-top sprinkled lightly with flour. Knead it gently with the fingertips to remove any cracks. Flatten into a 2.5cm (1-inch) thick disc. Wrap in foil or clingfilm (plastic wrap) and chill in the refrigerator for at least 30 minutes. (At this stage, it can be frozen for up to 3 months or refrigerated for 2 days.)

4. Choose a loose-bottomed flan tin or an oven-to-table dish, 23–25cm (9–10″) in diameter and 2.5–3cm (1–1¼″) deep.

5. Roll the chilled dough into a circle, then ease into the tin, pressing it well into the sides. Trim off any excess. Prick the case all over with a fork, then line with a piece of foil pressed into its shape. Freeze for at least 30 minutes.

6. Preheat the oven to 200°C (400°F/Gas 6).

7. Bake the frozen case for 10 minutes or until the pastry feels dry to the touch. Remove the foil and bake for a further 5 minutes until lightly browned, then remove from the oven.

8. Turn the oven down to 180°C (350°F/Gas 4).

9. Meanwhile, make the filling as follows. First cut the squash in half, then discard the seeds. To cook in a microwave,

cover each half with clingfilm (plastic wrap) punctured in 2
or 3 places and cook on 100 per cent power for 14 minutes.
To cook in a conventional oven, arrange the halves, cut-side
down, in a small roasting tin or casserole. Cook at 200°C
(400°F/Gas 6) for 45 minutes–1 hour.

10. In either case, test that it is done with a sharp pointed knife.
    If not tender, cook 2 minutes longer in a microwave or 20
    minutes longer in a conventional oven. Leave to cool.

11. Warm the olive oil in a heavy pan, then add the onion and
    cook slowly until it is melting but uncoloured. Scoop out the
    flesh of the squash from the skin and add to the onion.
    Continue to cook over low heat for 5 minutes, stirring well.

12. Put the eggs and cream in a mixing bowl. Add the pepper,
    salt and nutmeg and whisk together. Stir in the squash mix-
    ture and the cornflour (cornstarch) and mix thoroughly.
    Taste for seasonings, then pour into the pastry case. Smooth
    the surface, sprinkle with the cheese and bake for 40 min-
    utes.

13. Serve hot or warm.

Tourte à la Courge

When I was in Provence
researching the history of its
Jewish population in the Middle
Ages, I came across a dish quite
unknown to me which used
squash ('courge' in French) as
the filling for a savoury tourte. I
thought no more of it until I discovered that this vegetable –
and its near relation, the pumpkin – was a favourite Sukkot food
among many Sephardi communities. Had it reached Provence, I
wondered, via some of the Jews
fleeing from Spain and Portugal
in the 15th century?

Be that truth or fantasy,
Turkish Jews, at this time of the
year still make a flan with
squash or pumpkin called 'Flan
de Calabaza' – their name for the
vegetable which is called 'cal-
abassah' in Israel. Many
Sephardi communities also
make a savoury pumpkin
strudel.

There are no parallel recipes
among Ashkenazi Jews as the
climatic conditions in Europe –
certainly in Eastern Europe –
were not suitable for its cultiva-
tion. Now, however, squashes of
all kinds are available at green-
grocers in Britain.

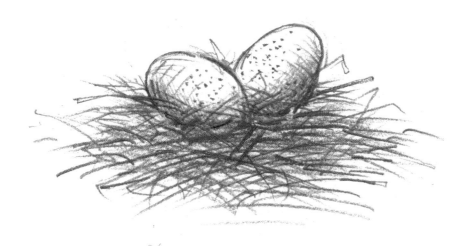

Savoury Beef Strudel with Apricots & Pine Kernels

Makes 2 strudels, each serving 3–4

Keeps in the refrigerator 2 days raw or 3 days cooked. Freeze raw 2 months.

1 x 450g (1 lb) pack puff
  pastry, thawed

For the meat mixture:
1 tbsp sunflower (canola)
  oil
50g (2oz/¼ cup) pine kernels
1 medium onion, peeled
  and finely chopped
1 fat clove of garlic, peeled
  and finely chopped
450g (1 lb) extra-lean
  minced (ground) beef
125g (4oz/¾ cup) tenderized
  dried apricots, quartered
1 tsp ground cumin
1 tbsp chopped parsley
¼ tsp ground nutmeg
1 tsp cinnamon
½ tsp sea salt
8 grinds of black pepper
4 tbsp meat
  or chicken stock

For the glaze:
1 whole egg, beaten
  (or 1 egg yolk with
  1 tsp cold water, beaten)
2 tbsp sesame seeds.

For best results, eat fresh from the oven. The juicy, spiced filling lends distinction to what is basically a family dish.

1. In a large sauté pan heat the oil, then fry the pine kernels until a rich gold. Remove from the pan and drain on paper towels.

2. In the same oil, cook the onions and the garlic over a medium heat until soft and golden, keeping the pan covered.

3. Add the meat and continue to cook, uncovered, breaking the meat up with a fork until it loses its pinkness.

4. Add all the remaining ingredients and bring to the boil.

5. Cover and simmer for 15 minutes until the meat feels tender when tasted. At this stage the mixture should be juicy, but with little free liquid. If too wet, continue to cook uncovered until this moisture disappears.

6. Taste and add a little extra salt if necessary, then stir in the pine kernels and spread the mixture on a flat dish to cool.

7. Preheat the oven to 220°C (425°F/Gas 7).

8. Divide the pastry in half and proceed with each half as follows. Roll each half into a rectangle 40 x 25cm (16 x 20″). It must be so thin that you can see the board through it.

9. Spread half the cooled meat over the pastry, leaving a 2.5cm (1″) margin all the way round. Turn the ends in to seal, then roll up like a flattened Swiss (jelly) roll.

10. Transfer to an ungreased baking tray, join-side down, then brush with the beaten egg. Sprinkle with the sesame seeds.

11. Make cuts 5–7cm (2–2½″) apart through the top layer of pastry to prevent the strudel bursting when cooked.

12. Bake for 10 minutes, then turn the oven down to 200°C (400°F/Gas 6) for a further 15–20 minutes, until crisp and brown.

13. Serve warm.

Chilled Melon Soup with a Swirl of Raspberry

Serves 6   (photograph between pages 56 and 57)

Keeps 3 days in the refrigerator without the raspberries.

A wonderful fruity Sukkot soup, ideal to serve on a sunny 'Indian Summer' day.

1. In a small saucepan, dissolve 25g (1oz/2 tbsp) of the sugar in the water, then bubble uncovered for 5 minutes and leave to cool.

2. Halve the melon(s) and discard the seeds. Using a melon baller or a dessert spoon, scoop out the flesh, and purée in a food processor, together with the wine.

3. Add the sugar syrup and lime juice, pulse several times until evenly mixed, then pour into a bowl or container. Refrigerate.

4. Meanwhile purée the raspberries in the food processor with the remaining sugar. Push through a sieve, using the bowl of a soup ladle as a 'pusher', to remove the seeds.

5. To serve, ladle the soup into individual soup bowls, then swirl the purée through each serving to give a marbled effect. Top each one with a little of the lime zest.

50g (2oz/¼ cup) granulated sugar
400 ml (14 floz/1¾ cups) water
1 large ripe Galia melon or two small melons, 1.5kg (3¼ lb) total weight
250 ml (9 floz/1 cup + 2 tbsp) white wine
juice and grated zest of 1 lime
225g (8oz/1 cup) raspberries (frozen or fresh)

Chilled Melon Soup

This is a most unusual and refreshing cold soup. However, what makes it outstanding is a purée of raspberries marbled through the soup.

Don't expect to get a memorable flavour as soon as it is made – It's quite different after 24 hours. And when we finished it off 3 days later, it was still brilliant! However, I wouldn't freeze it, as the melon flavour is too delicate for prolonged storage.

Meat-Stuffed Vine Leaves

Serves 6–8. Makes about 24   (photograph between pages 56 and 57)

125g (4oz/¾ cup)
   long grain (Patna or
   Basmati) rice
1 vacuum pack (225 g/8oz)
   vine leaves in brine
1 medium onion, peeled
   and finely chopped
2 tbsp sunflower
   (canola) oil
225g (8oz) lean minced
   (ground) beef or lamb
scant tsp salt
10 grinds of black pepper
2 tsp dried mint (optional)
½ tsp each mixed spice and
   cinnamon
3 peeled garlic cloves,
   cut in slivers

For the sauce:
4 tbsp extra virgin olive oil
150 ml (5 floz/⅔ cup) chick-
   en stock
4 tbsp lemon juice
1½ tbsp sugar

Leaves, stuffed and ready to cook, can be frozen for 1 month, cooked leftovers 3 months. Stuffed and cooked leaves will keep 3 days in the refrigerator.

Although it is traditional to serve these hot, I think the flavour comes through more clearly when they are served chilled or at room temperature. They are equally suitable to serve as a starter or as a main dish with another kind of stuffed vegetable or leaf.

Note: Vacuum packs of vine leaves can be found at most health food shops and delis. They have a shelf life of a year!

1. Preheat the oven to 150°F (300°F/Gas 2).

2. Put the rice in a sieve, then stand this in a bowl and pour on boiling water to cover. Leave to soak.

3. Meanwhile, put the vine leaves in another bowl and cover them with boiling water. When they are cool enough to han-dle, first separate them, then lay them in a colander and rinse with cold water. Leave to drain.

4. Sauté the chopped onion in the sunflower oil until soft and golden, then put into a bowl with the meat and all the sea-sonings.

5. Rinse the rice under the cold tap. Drain well, then add to the bowl and mix with a fork until well blended.

6. Arrange any torn leaves in a layer on the bottom of a 20cm (8-inch) casserole. To stuff the leaves spread them out on a board, vein-side up, with the stalk end towards you. Place a heaped teaspoon of filling towards the stalk end of each leaf, then turn in the sides and roll up into a tight little parcel, rather like a fat cigar.

7. Lay each stuffed leaf in turn in the palm of your hand and squeeze it lightly to seal it. Then arrange the parcels in two layers, tucking slivers of garlic into each layer.

8. To make the sauce, mix together the oil, chicken stock, lemon juice and sugar and pour carefully over the stuffed leaves. Lay a small plate on top to keep them tightly rolled, then cover with the casserole lid or a piece of foil.

9. Cook for 3 hours, or until the leaves are quite tender – by this time the cooking liquid will have been almost completely absorbed.

10. Serve warm or refrigerate.

Meat Stuffed Vineleaves

Hot or cold, vine leaves stuffed with a spiced mixture of minced meat and rice are truly a dish to swoon over. However, it's important to cook them very slowly, for up to 3 hours. Originally this was done in a pan on top of the stove, but it is much less demanding when cooked in the oven as there is no chance of the vine leaves catching on the bottom of the pan. By the end of the cooking time, the sauce should have been absorbed by the rice in the stuffing.

Aubergine, Pepper & Tomato Ragout

Serves 6

Keeps 4 days in the refrigerator. Do not freeze.

2 medium glossy aubergines
(eggplants), unpeeled
and cut into 1.5cm
($\frac{5}{8}$-inch) cubes
3 tbsp olive oil
1 large onion, peeled, halved,
then sliced paper-thin
3 yellow or orange peppers
(bell peppers), seeded,
cored, then cut into strips
1.5cm ($\frac{5}{8}$ inch) wide and
5cm (2″) long
1 fat clove of garlic, peeled
and finely chopped
1 x 400g (14oz) can chopped
tomatoes
2 tsp tomato purée (paste)
1 tsp dried herbes de
Provence
1 tsp salt
15 grinds of black pepper
good pinch of sugar

For garnish:
1 tbsp chopped parsley.

A particularly successful combination of flavours – mouth-watering, in fact. Serve warm as a vegetable or at room temperature as a starter. Allow the flavours to develop by making the ragoût one day, or even two, before it is to be served.

1. Soak the aubergine cubes in a bowl of water with 2 tsp salt. After 30 minutes, squeeze as dry as possible, then pat dry with paper towels.

2. Meanwhile, in a large lidded sauté or heavy frying pan, heat the oil and cook the onion until soft and golden.

3. Add the aubergines and fry until lightly browned, then add the pepper strips and the garlic and cook gently for another 5 minutes.

4. Add the chopped tomatoes, tomato purée, herbs and seasonings. Cover and simmer for 15 minutes until the vegetables are tender. This mixture should be a thick stew. If too thin, bubble uncovered for 5 minutes.

5. Stir in the parsley and serve warm or at room temperature.

Aubergine, Pepper & Tomato Ragout

The aubergine comes in many shapes and colours – pink, purple and even a white variety which is egg-shaped, hence its American name, 'egg-plant'. The Israeli-grown aubergine was the first to appear in Britain some 25 years ago, but since then it has been developed and marketed by many other countries, Holland, in particular.

The new varieties seem to have less of the bitter juices of the earlier ones. The aubergines presently coming into Britain have a sweet creamy flesh when cooked, as well as very few seeds.

This sweetness is particularly noticeable when cubes of aubergines are cooked together with peppers and onion in a herb-flavoured tomato sauce. This mélange makes a wonderful accompaniment to grilled lamb chops. Because it's cooked in olive oil, it's equally delicious served at room temperature, either as a starter, with plenty of good bread to mop up the juices, or as a relish to serve with cold chicken or meat. In this particular version, I have cut the amount of oil dramatically, without affecting the flavour.

Stuffed Aubergines in an Apricot Sauce

Serves 8 (photograph between pages 56 and 57)

Keeps 3 days in the refrigerator. Freeze 3 months.

The combination of the sweet-fleshed aubergine and the dried fruit balanced by the tartness of fresh lemon juice is quite magical. Serve the dish with rice or, for a contrast of textures, with tiny roast potatoes. Don't rush the cooking – the timing I give is essential for the development of the unique flavour.

1. Preheat the oven to 160°C (325°F/Gas 3).

2. Cut each aubergine in half lengthways, then scoop out the inside with a spoon, leaving 1.25cm (½ inch) of flesh next to the skin. Coarsely chop the scooped-out flesh, either in the food processor or with a knife.

3. Heat the oil in a large lidded frying pan. Add the chopped aubergine, stir well, then cover and cook gently until absolutely tender – about 10 minutes.

4. In the food processor (or a blender) purée the onion and the bread (both cut into roughly 2.5cm/1-inch chunks) together with the egg and seasonings.

5. Add to the raw mince in a large bowl, together with the cooked aubergine flesh (removed from the pan with a slotted spoon) Mix with a large fork until well blended.

6. Divide the meat mixture between the aubergine halves, pressing it down firmly.

7. Reheat the oil left in the pan (add an extra spoonful if necessary), then fry the stuffed aubergines, meat-side down, until a rich brown – at which point they will come away easily from the pan. Turn over and fry the second side briefly, then lay side by side in a roasting tin or casserole.

4 boat-shaped aubergines
(eggplants)
(225–300g/8–10oz each)
3 tbsp olive oil

For the meat mixture:
1 medium onion
1 thick slice of bread
1 egg
1 scant tsp salt
15 grinds of black pepper
675g (1½ lb) lean minced
(ground) beef

For the sauce:
1 x 250g (9oz) pack ready-
to-eat dried apricots
4 level tbsp demerara or
golden granulated sugar
2 tbsp lemon juice

**Stuffed Aubergines
in apricot Sauce
continued**

8. Pour 225 ml (8 floz/1 cup) of hot water into the frying
pan and stir well to release any tasty bits on the bottom.
Add the dried apricots, then pour this around the
aubergines. Sprinkle with half the sugar, then cover with
foil or a lid and bake for 1½ hours.

9. Uncover and baste with the juices, then sprinkle with the
remaining sugar and the lemon juice. Continue to cook
slowly for a further 30 minutes, still uncovered, to allow the
sauce to thicken to a syrupy consistency. If too dry, add a little more water.

10. Taste and add more sugar or lemon juice if necessary,
then serve.

Stuffed Aubergines with an Apricot Sauce

Until recently, the aubergine was unfamiliar to most Ashkenazi cooks.
The exceptions were those families with roots in Romania – and therein
lies the clue to the past history of this most versatile of vegetables.

Romania was once part of the Ottoman Empire, and for the finest
aubergine recipes, we must look to the cuisine of Sephardi Jews from the
former Turkish Empire, which included at its height Greece, Syria, the
Lebanon and Egypt.

The story of the progress of the aubergine from its birthplace in a
remote part of Asia to its present importance in international cuisine is
most graphically revealed by the evolution of its name. Its original name,
the Sanskrit 'vatinganah' (the translation of which describes its effect on
the digestion – to put it politely) became 'badingan' in Persian, and then
'al-badhinjan' in Arabic.

When the Arabic-speaking Moors occupied Spain early in the 8th century, they brought the aubergine with them. The native Spanish cooks,
hearing the Arabic word, but not being able to read it, called it
'alberginia'.

The French in their turn produced a Gallic version of the Spanish word
and so it became – and has remained – the 'aubergine'. However, if you
are looking for aubergine recipes in the Sephardi cuisine that has its ori-
gins in Spain and Portugal, you will have to look it up under 'Berencena'
or 'Berenjenna' – its name in Ladino, the Spanish equivalent of Yiddish –
which is a synthesis of its Arabic and Spanish names.

*Opposite: chicken soup (page 3)
Over left: butternut squash and apple soup (page 19)
Over right: salmon steaks with avocado salsa (page 20)
Centre left: apple and ginger lekach (page 30)
with marillen (page 33)
Centre right: herring salad (page 41)*

Dried Fruit Strudel with Flaky Cream Cheese Pastry

Makes 20 slices

Keeps 1 week in an airtight container. Freeze 3 months.

A melt-in-the-mouth flaky pastry encloses a juicy filling of spicy vine fruits and nuts.

1. The day before baking, put the dried fruit mixture in a large bowl. Add the grated apple, sugar, walnuts and spices and mix well. Leave in the kitchen overnight to mature.

2. To make the pastry, use butter which is the consistency of Plasticine – pliable but not spreadable. Work it together with the curd cheese, either with a wooden spoon or a mixer fitted with a 'K' beater. Gradually work in the flour and icing sugar until a dough is formed. Knead lightly with the fingers until smooth.

3. Divide in two and flatten each portion into a 2.5cm (1″) thick disc. Wrap each in foil and refrigerate overnight.

4. When ready to assemble, preheat the oven to 220°C (425°F/Gas 7).

5. Work on each portion of pastry as follows. On a floured board, roll out thinly to a 22.5 x 30cm (9 x 12″) rectangle. Spread with half the jam and then with half the fruit mixture, leaving a clear 2.5cm (1″) border all the way round. Turn in the short sides, then roll up across the 30cm (12-inch) width into a strudel.

6. Place on a baking tray with the join underneath. Make cuts 2.5cm (1″) apart through the top layer of pastry – this helps to prevent cracking.

7. Bake for 5 minutes, then turn the heat down to 190°C (375°F/Gas 5) and cook for a further 20 minutes until the strudels are a rich brown.

8. Slice right through the cuts as soon as the strudels come out of the oven (this prevents crumbling), then cool on a rack.

9. Before serving, dust the slices with icing sugar.

For the pastry:
125g (4oz/½ cup) butter
125g (4oz/½ cup curd
  (smooth cottage) cheese
125g (4oz/1 cup) self-raising
  flour (or plain (all-purpose) flour with 1 level
  tsp baking powder)
1 tbsp icing (powdered)
  sugar

For the filling:
1 x 250g (9oz) pack (1½
  cups) luxury mixed dried
  fruit
1 small eating apple, grated
2 tbsp light Muscovado
  sugar
1 x 100g (3½oz) pack (1
  cup) walnut pieces
1 tsp cinnamon
1 tsp mixed sweet spice
4 tbsp apricot jam

To dust the slices:
icing (powdered) sugar

Previous left: melon soup (page 48)
Previous right: meat-stuffed vine leaves (page 52)
    and stuffed aubergines (page 54)
Opposite: pineapple blitz torte (page 63)

A Fresh Peach & Macaroon Strudel

Serves 8

The strudel will keep 2 days in the refrigerator and may be reheated in a moderate oven until warm to the touch. Freeze leftovers 2 weeks

6 large firm peaches (about 900 g/2 lb)
4 tbsp caster (superfine) sugar
2 tsp fresh lemon juice
3 tbsp brandy or Amaretto (almond-flavoured liqueur)
1 x 85–100g (3¼–3½oz pack of macaroons or Amaretti biscuits, crumbled
6 tbsp granulated sugar
6 sheets filo (phyllo) pastry
50–75g (2–3oz/¼–⅓ cup) unsalted butter or block margarine, melted
icing (powdered) sugar

An inspired combination of fruit and flavour.

1. Cut the fruit away from the stones (pits) in 1.5cm (1½") thick slices. Place in a bowl and sprinkle with the caster sugar, lemon juice and the brandy or liqueur. Allow to stand for at least 30 minutes to soak up the juices.

2. Preheat the oven to 200°C (400°F/Gas 6).

3. Crush the biscuits with a rolling pin until like coarse sand, then mix with the granulated sugar.

4. Have 6 sheets of filo pastry arranged under a tea (dish) towel.

5. Cut 2 of the sheets in half vertically, and use these to overlap each of the 4 full sheets to widen them. Each sheet should then be approximately 45cm (18") wide.

6. Lay one of the enlarged sheets on a tea towel, then brush lightly with melted butter or margarine. Cover with another of the enlarged sheets, then brush with melted butter or margarine and sprinkle evenly with half of the biscuit crumbs.

7. Repeat with another sheet of enlarged pastry, brushing with butter or margarine and sprinkle with a quarter of the biscuit crumbs.

8. Repeat with the last enlarged sheet, scattering with the remaining biscuit crumbs.

9. Lift the peach slices out of the marinade with a slotted spoon. Arrange in a line about 10cm (4″) from the edge of the pastry nearest to you, but leaving an inch of pastry clear of fruit at either side. Spoon a tablespoon of the remaining marinade on top of the fruit.

10. Turn the sides of the pastry in to seal in the juices, then roll up into a strudel and place on a well greased shallow baking tray. Brush the top of the strudel with a little melted fat, then mark into about 8 slices, cutting through only the top layer.

11. Bake for 25–30 minutes until crisp and golden brown.

Note: If juice runs out of the strudel during the baking time, spoon it on top of the baked pastry. It will then set into a glaze.

12. Serve in slices, either warm or at room temperature, sprinkled with a layer of icing (powdered) sugar.

Mango & Crystallized Ginger Slice

Serves 8

Keeps 2 days under refrigeration. Freeze 2 months.

For the almond pastry:
250g (9oz/2¼ cups) plain
  (all-purpose) flour
pinch of salt
25g (1oz/¼ cup)
  ground almonds
  or hazelnuts
75g (3oz/⅓ cup)
  caster (superfine) sugar
175g (6oz/¾ cup) butter or
  firm margarine, cut into
  2.5cm (1-inch) chunks
1 egg yolk
2 tbsp single
  (light) cream or milk
  (water for a meat meal)

For the filling:
25g (1oz/¼ cup)
  ground almonds
75g (3oz/ light
  muscovado sugar
1 tbsp cornflour
  (cornstarch)
2 tsp finely grated
  lemon rind
3 large ripe mangoes
  (900g/2lb total weight),
  peeled and thinly sliced
  from the stone (pit)
50g (2oz/⅓ cup) chopped
  crystallized (candied)
  ginger or tsp ground ginger
1 tbsp lemon juice

The melt-in-the-mouth Viennese-style pastry blends to perfection with the juicy filling.

1. Make the pastry 2 hours in advance – this is made in seconds in a food processor, or use the rubbing-in method, either by hand or machine. Put the dry ingredients and the well-chilled chunks of fat into the bowl with the egg yolk and liquid, then pulse until the mixture looks like a very moist crumble. Tip into a bowl and gather into a ball.

2. Turn the pastry on to a board or counter-top sprinkled with a very light layer of flour. Knead it gently with the fingertips to remove any cracks, then flatten into a disc about 2.5cm (1-inch) thick. Chill one half and freeze the rest for 1–1½ hours (both wrapped in foil).

3. Preheat the oven to 190°C (375°F/Gas 5). Put in a baking tray to heat.

4. Roll out the chilled pastry to fit either a 22cm (8¾″) square loose-bottomed flan tin or a baking tin approximately 27.5 x 17.5 x 2cm (11 x 7 x ¾″). If the pastry is very firm, work with the hands so it can be rolled out easily. Sprinkle with the ground almonds.

5. Mix the sugar, cornflour (cornstarch) and lemon rind in a bowl and gently fold in the slices of fruit and the crystallized ginger or the ground ginger.

6. Turn into the prepared tin in an even layer and sprinkle with the lemon juice.

7. Grate the frozen pastry coarsely in an even layer over the fruit and scatter with the mixed nuts and sugar.

8. Carefully lay the tin with the unbaked slice on the hot baking tray and bake for 40 minutes, or until a rich golden brown.

9. To serve, cut in slices and serve at room temperature, plain or with creamy fromage frais or Greek yoghurt lightly sweetened with runny honey, or with parev ice-cream after a meat meal.

For the topping:
the frozen pastry
2 tbsp chopped pecans or
  walnuts
1 tbsp golden granulated
  sugar

Mango & Crystallized Ginger Slice

A ripe mango will give all over when gently pressed with the fingertips. Once fully ripe, it will keep for 4 or 5 days in the refrigerator. If good peaches are available, an equal weight can be used instead of the mango.

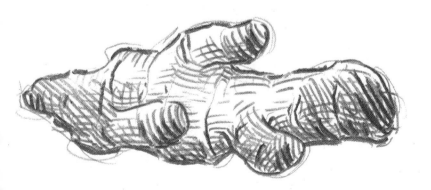

61

Apfelkuchen Squares

Makes 24 squares

Keeps 3 days in the refrigerator. Freeze 3 months.

225g (8oz/2 cups)
  self raising flour (or plain
  (all purpose) flour with 2
  level tsp baking powder)
175g (6oz/¾ cup)
  soft margarine or butter
125g (4oz/½ cup) caster
  (superfine) sugar
grated rind of half a lemon
3 eggs
900g (2 lb) baking apples
  (weight when peeled and
  cored), thinly sliced
t tbsp granulated sugar
2 tbsp lemon juice
2 rounded tbsp apricot jam

For the topping:
50g (2oz/½ cup)
  walnuts, finely chopped
50g (2oz/¼ cup)
  demerara sugar

A juicy layer of apple slices is sandwiched between a sponge base and a crunchy walnut topping. The squares can be briefly reheated either in a microwave or in a hot oven.

1. Preheat the oven to 180°C (350°F/Gas 4). Grease a tin measuring approximately 30 x 20 x 4cm (12 x 8 x 1½").

2. Put the flour, fat, caster sugar, lemon rind and eggs into a bowl and beat by hand, mixer or food processor until smooth.

3. Spread two-thirds of the mixture thinly over the base of the tin.

4. Arrange the sliced apples in an even layer on top, sprinkle with granulated sugar and lemon juice and dot with the jam.

5. Drop the remaining cake mixture by teaspoonfuls all over the apple filling and put in the oven.

6. After 10 minutes, open the oven, quickly smooth the blobs of cake mixture over the top of the apples with a large fork, then sprinkle evenly with the mixed nuts and demerara sugar.

7. Close the oven and bake for a further 30 minutes, or until the cake is golden-brown and the apples feel tender when pierced with a sharp knife.

8. Cut into 5cm (2-inch) squares to serve.

Pineapple Blitz Torte

Serves 10–12 (photograph between pages 56 and 57)

Keeps 3 days under refrigeration. Complete cake freezes 1 month.

Delicate layers of sponge are topped with meringue before baking, then filled with a mouth-watering combination of fruit, liqueur and cream.

1. Preheat the oven to 180°C (350°F/Gas 4). Grease 2 x 24cm (9½ inch) loose-bottomed sandwich or spring-form tins, and line the base with circles of silicone liner or greaseproof (wax) paper.

2. Cream the butter and sugar until fluffy. Beat in the yolks and liquid, then fold in the flour. Divide between the prepared tins and smooth level (the layers will be thin).

3. For the meringue, whisk the whites until they hold floppy peaks, then add the 200g (7oz/1 cup) sugar a tablespoonful at a time, whisking until stiff peaks are formed after each addition.

4. Spread evenly over each layer of cake mixture, then scatter with the almonds and cinnamon sugar.

5. Bake for 30 minutes or until the meringue is lightly browned and crisp to the touch.

6. Cool for 30 minutes, then ease on to wire racks.

7. To glaze the pineapple, dissolve the sugar and water in a wide, shallow pan. Then add the pineapple in one layer and cook until only 2 tablespoons syrup remains in the pan and the pineapple is beginning to caramelize.

8. Lift out the pineapple with a slotted spoon. Drain the fruit well, reserving the syrup and adding to it the Amaretto, rum or orange juice.

9. Whip the cream until it hangs on the whisk. Add the lemon juice and the remaining syrup and liqueur or orange juice, then whisk until it stands in firm peaks. Stir in the pineapple and chill well.

For the cake:
150g (5oz/⅔ cup) soft butter or margarine
150g (5oz/⅔ cup) caster (superfine) sugar
5 egg yolks
2 tbsp milk or water
125g (4oz/1 cup) sponge self-raising flour (or plain (all purpose) flour with 1 level tsp baking powder)

For the meringue:
5 egg whites
200g (7oz/scant 1 cup) caster (superfine) sugar
50g (2oz/½ cup) flaked almonds
2 tsp granulated sugar mixed with ½ tsp cinnamon

For the filling:
125g (4oz/½ cup) granulated sugar
200 ml (7 floz/¾ cup plus 2 tbsp) water
1 large pineapple, peeled, cored and sliced, then cut into 1cm (½-inch) wide segments
4 tbsp Amaretto liqueur, rum or orange juice
300 ml (10 floz/1¼ cups) whipping cream or 225–250 ml (8–9 floz/generous 1 cup) non-dairy cream
2 tbsp lemon juice

Pineapple Blitz Torte
continued

10. To assemble, put one layer, meringue side down, on a plate. Spread evenly with the fruit and cream and top with the other layer, meringue-side up.

11. Serve chilled.

Palace Pastries with a Three-Nut Filling

Makes 20–22

Keep 1 week in the refrigerator. Freeze 3 months.

225g (8oz) puff pastry sheet

For the filling:
175g (6oz/1½ cups)
  blanched almonds
75g (3oz/¾ cup) natural pistachios, shelled
75g (3oz/¾ cup) white
  sesame seeds
40g (1½oz/3 tbsp) butter or
  margarine
½ tsp mixed sweet spice
3 tsp citrus-blossom water
2 tsp rose-water
1 egg white
40g (1½oz/3 tbsp) caster
  (superfine) sugar

A variation on baklava, but using the easy-to-handle puff pastry instead of filo (phyllo) pastry. Delicious served with stewed fruit or with coffee.

1. Preheat the oven to 190°C (375°F/Gas 5). Grease a roulade or Swiss (jelly) roll tin about 30 x 20 x 2.5cm (12 x 8 x 1″).

2. First make the filling. Using the pulse action, chop the almonds and pistachios until fine but still with some texture.

3. Sauté with the sesame seeds in the butter or margarine until golden, stirring constantly.

4. Turn into a bowl and stir in the spice, citrus-blossom water and rose-water.

5. Whisk the egg white until it holds stiff peaks, then whisk in the sugar a teaspoonful at a time. Add to the nut mixture and mix thoroughly.

6. Roll out the pastry sheet until it is as thin as possible – it should be 40cm (16″) wide.

7. Spread three-quarters of the pastry with the filling, leaving the quarter of pastry furthest away from you quite bare. Then roll up into a tight Swiss (jelly) roll, finishing with the join underneath.

8. Cut the roll into 20–22 slices, each rather more than 1.25cm (½ inch) thick. Then lay the slices side by side, without touching, in the tin.

9. Bake for 30 minutes or until the slices are golden brown.

10. Prepare the syrup as soon as the pastries go into the oven as it must be allowed to cool to room temperature. Put the sugar and water into a medium-sized pan and heat, stirring, until the sugar has dissolved.

11. Add the lemon juice and bubble gently for about 12 minutes until the syrup will thickly coat the back of a wooden spoon. Then stir in the citrus-blossom water and rose-water and leave – as it cools, it will thicken to the consistency of thin honey. If too thick, add a little boiling water and stir well.

12. When the pastries come out of the oven, leave them in the tin for 5 minutes to cool. Then pour the syrup over them and allow it to soak in for 2 hours, basting once or twice.

13. Serve at room temperature with the bottom of each roll to the top, each one lightly scattered with pistachios.

For the syrup:
225g (8oz/1 cup) granulated sugar
175 ml (6 floz/¾ cup) water
1 tbsp lemon juice
1 tbsp citrus-blossom water
2 tsp rose-water

For the garnish:
2 tbsp coarsely chopped pistachios

Etrog (Citron) Three-Fruit Marmalade

Keeps 9 months in the refrigerator, 2 years in the freezer

Makes about 1kg (2?1/4 1b).

1 etrog
1 large orange
1 grapefruit
150 ml (5 floz/⅔ cup) orange
   juice
jam sugar with pectin equal
   to the total weight of
   the fruit

Etrog (Citron)
Three-Fruit Marmalade

Marmalade does not
exhaust the possible uses of
this wonderful fruit after it has
been part of the Sukkot cere-
monials. Should you be visit-
ing Israel, you will find crystallized etrog peel on sale in Mea
Sharim. If, however, Corsica is
on your holiday schedule, do
look out for a delicious etrog
liqueur   (Cedrat-Citron).
Although it is very sweet, it
packs a powerful alcoholic
punch, containing 35 per cent
of alcohol.

You can often buy reduced
price etrogim which are
unsuitable for religious pur-
poses because of some imper-
fection, but which are fine for
cooking.

This has a wonderful bitter-sweet flavour. Using jam sugar with
pectin already added makes it set very quickly. However, once
the sugar has been added, the peel will not soften any more, so
do cook it until it's absolutely tender, as directed.

1. Wash the fruit and cut in half. Squeeze the juice from the
   orange and grapefruit (there's none in the etrog).

2. Scrape out the pulp and most of the pith. Put only the pulp
   with any pips in a bag made from muslin or half a yellow J-
   cloth tied with string.

3. Slice the peel very finely with a sharp knife (it's not worth
   using a food processor).

4. Put the shredded peel in a 22.5cm (9-inch) heavy pan,
   together with the juice from the fruit, the orange juice and
   enough water barely to cover the fruit. Add the muslin bag.

5. Cover and cook at a slow simmer for about 2 hours until the
   peel is absolutely tender (this process takes only 10–15 minutes at 15lb pressure in a pressure cooker).

6. Remove the muslin bag and squeeze (wearing rubber gloves)
   to extract any juice.

7. Now add the sugar. Stir over a moderate heat until it dissolves, then bring to a fast rolling boil and cook until setting
   point is reached – after about 10 minutes.

To test for setting point:

8. The flake test (the one I use): catch a little jam in the bowl of the wooden spoon. Lift it above the pan and allow it to cool for a minute. Turn the spoon so that the marmalade drops from the edge. If the marmalade has reached setting point, the drops of jam will run together to form a flake which breaks off cleanly and sharply from the spoon. Marmalade which runs off in a liquid stream or separate droplets needs further boiling.

Potting and storing the marmalade:

9. place the required number of clean, hot jars (heated for 10 minutes at 120°C (250°F/Gas 1/2), with rubber rings inset in the lid, on a heat proof surface. Use a ladle to fill them to the top through a jam funnel, then screw down the lid.

10. Keep in a cool cupboard

Hanukkah
The Festival of Lights

This joyous Festival celebrates the victory of good over evil, and the saving of the Jewish people from a tyrant's wicked plans. In the second century BCE the Jewish warrior Judas Maccabeus won a famous victory over the occupying forces of Antiochus IV, who had desecrated the Temple in Jerusalem with pagan rites. Judas's father was at the time High Priest of Israel and he inspired his sons to do battle with the Greeks.

After the Greeks had been driven from the Temple, the Jewish soldiers discovered that there was only enough undefiled oil to allow the Sacred Menorah (the many-branched candelabra) to burn for one day 'it would take eight days for more oil to be prepared'. But then, as every Jewish child knows, a miracle occurred and the Menorah stayed alight for eight days, an 'everlasting light'.

It's very much a family Festival as everyone gathers round their own Menorah when an extra candle is lit on each of the eight days. After the blessings are said in honour of the Festival, both young and old all join in singing the rousing hymn of praise 'Maoz Tsur' – Rock of Ages.

For two millennia, Hanukkah has been celebrated by cooking and eating foods that are fried in oil or contain it. Another custom that has grown up over the centuries is that of 'Hanukkah Gelt' (money) being given to the children of the family.

Amongst all the rich goodies that are traditional, the one dish that is universal in the Ashkenazi cuisine at this Festival is the 'latke'. In Britain, latkes are invariably made with grated potatoes and onions, but in the USA, the Jewish community will have a dozen different varieties including carrot, spinach, corn, cauliflower, mixed vegetables and cinnamon-flavoured potato.

In Britain in the last hundred years it has become the custom to make a steamed Hanukkah fruit pudding, and a Hanukkah fruit cake at this season. And in recent years, as kosher ones have become more plentiful, a fine roast turkey with both a helzel and a chestnut stuffing has increasingly graced Hanukkah tables.

A delicious Sephardi dish of the season is the Hanukkah Kibbeh – a unique mixture of bulgur (cracked wheat) and savoury meat. This is cooked in a flat dish, rather like a pie, instead of the traditionaltorpedo-shaped delicacies that you really need to learn how to make at your mother's knee.

In recent years, Sufganiyot (doughnuts, Israeli-style) have become more popular. The Hungarian ones in this chapter are superb, combining the German-Jewish traditional 'krapfen' (fritters) with the 'bimuelos' (deep-fried puffs soaked in syrup) of the Sephardi tradition.

As you can see, Hanukkah is one Festival where the rules of healthy eating are temporarily suspended! But for these eight days in the year let us celebrate and drink a glass of Hot Spiced Wine Cup, in tribute to Judas Maccabeus and his brothers and their famous victory more than two thousand years ago.

Classic Potato Latkes

Serves 4–6. Makes 12–13 large latkes   (photograph between pages 120 and 121)

Best served hot off the pan. The cooked latkes keep 2 days in the refrigerator. Freeze 4 months.

3 large baking potatoes,
   peeled
   (about 675 g/1½
lb) – enough to fill a
   600-ml (1-pint/2½ cup)
   measure when grated
1 medium (200 g/7oz)
   onion, peeled
4 level tbsp self-raising flour
   with ½ tsp of baking powder (or 4 level tbsp plain
   (all-purpose) flour with 1
   tsp baking powder)
1 level tsp salt
speck of white pepper
2 eggs
any flavourless oil for frying

Crunchy on the outside, almost creamy inside – each year's batch is just that little bit different, but that's half the pleasure.

1. You can grate the potatoes and onion by hand in the tradi-tional way or, preferably, use a food processor.

Using a food processor:
2. With many grating discs the potato pulp will be too coarse, so it's advisable to pulse it briefly as well, using the metal blade (see below). Cut the potatoes and peeled onion to fit the feed tube, then grate through the grating disc. Turn into a bowl, then change to the metal blade. Put the potato/onion mixture back in the processor and pulse 4 times.

With either method:
3. Turn into a metal sieve and press down firmly with a spoon to remove as much moisture as possible. Leave to drain fur-ther whilst you prepare the batter.

4. If you want to keep one batch hot whilst you cook the sec-ond, preheat the oven to 180°C (350°F/Gas 4).

5. Put the flour, baking powder and seasonings into a mixing bowl, then add the beaten eggs gradually, stirring until you have a batter. Add the drained potato and onions and mix thoroughly.

6. Put oil to a depth of 1cm (½ inch) into a 22cm (9-inch) heavy frying pan. Heat until a little of the potato mixture sizzles when it is put into the pan.

7. Put tablespoons of the mixture into the pan, flattening them slightly with the back of the spoon. Cook over a moderate heat with the oil gently but continuously bubbling round them until the underside is a rich brown (after 3–4 minutes). Then turn over carefully and fry the second side in the same way.

8. Drain on crumpled paper towels, then transfer to a serving dish and either eat hot from the pan or keep hot in the oven for up to 15 minutes.

9. If you plan to cook the latkes in advance, drain, and then open-freeze them before storing them in bags.

10. To reheat, arrange the frozen latkes on baking trays and heat in a hot oven 230°C (450°F/Gas 8) for 6–7 minutes or until crisp to the touch and piping hot.

Potato Latkes

Terrible culinary sins are sometimes committed when making latkes. We've all experienced them at one time or another: stodgy, rather than creamy insides; soggy instead of crunchy outsides; and the cardinal sin of all which most of us commit at some time or another – not making enough! Alas, I can't tell you how to avoid the last one – as with tsimmes, the family's capacity for latkes is infinite. However, there are a few ground rules that can help in avoiding the other two.

Stodginess is usually due to not draining enough liquid from the raw onion and potato and then having to add extra 'binder' – whether flour or matzo meal – to achieve the right texture. Sogginess means a fault in the frying, usually caused by starting to fry the latkes in oil that is too cool and so is absorbed into the mixture instead of creating a crisp coating on the outside. However, if the oil's too hot, then the outside browns before the inside is cooked and we're back to sogginess again. So the rule is to heat the oil until a teaspoon of the mixture dropped into it makes a satisfying sizzling sound. Then when the latkes have been placed in the oil, turn down the heat until the oil is just bubbling lazily round each one. I reckon it should take 3–4 minutes on each side to achieve a really crunchy crust and a really creamy interior.

When it comes to the actual recipe, it's a brave cook who claims to have the best – that accolade belongs to the one that you, I and every other Jewish cook make for the family each Hanukkah.

A Succulent Roast Turkey for Hanukkah

Serves 11–12

7kg (15 lb) turkey

For the turkey stock:
the giblets
1 large carrot, peeled
    and cut into 4
1 medium onion, peeled
1.75 litres
    (3 pints/7½ cups) water
1 tsp black peppercorns
1 bay leaf
1 tsp salt

To put into the body cavity:
salt
pepper
large bunch of parsley
1 large apple, cut into 8

olive oil for brushing
    the bird

For the basting sauce:
125 ml (4 floz/½ cup) sunflower
    (canola) oil
125g (4oz/½ cup) margarine
125 ml (4 floz/½ cup) orange juice
2 tbsp fresh lemon juice

For the gravy:
1½ tbsp cornflour (cornstarch)
75 ml (3 floz/⅓ cup) dry vermouth
    or sherry
600 ml (1 pint/2½ cups) strained
    turkey stock
salt
black pepper

Carefully follow the instructions in this recipe and you can be assured of a perfectly cooked bird every time.

For a smaller bird, cook for the first 15 minutes as given below, then cook for 15 minutes per 450g (1 lb). For a larger bird, allow 12 minutes per 450g (1 lb).

1. To make the stock: on the day before the turkey is to be cooked, put the giblets (except for the liver) into a pan with the vegetables, water and seasonings. Simmer, uncovered, over a low heat, for 2 hours.

2. Alternatively, in a microwave use 725 ml (1¼ pints/ 3 cups) water and cook, covered, on 100 per cent power for 15 minutes – until bubbling – then cook on 50 per cent power for a further 20 minutes.

3. Strain the stock and chill overnight, then remove any fat.

4. The night before cooking , pat the bird dry inside and out, then lightly season the body cavity with salt and pepper and put in the parsley and apple sections.

5. Stuff the neck loosely with the helzel stuffing (p. 74) and sew it closed. Tie the drumsticks together. Brush the bird all over with a thin layer of olive oil.

6. Meanwhile, put the oil and melted fat for the basting sauce into a bowl, and in it soak a piece of butter muslin (cheesecloth) or a scalded large J-cloth (or two) big enough to cover the bird.

7. Cover the turkey completely with the fat-soaked cloth, tucking it well in all the way round to ensure that no flesh is exposed. Refrigerate or leave in a cool place overnight.

8. Next day, assuming you want to serve the turkey at 2 pm, take it from the refrigerator at 9.45 am and preheat the oven to 220°C (425°F/Gas 7).

9. At 10 am set the bird on a rack in a roasting tin and roast for 15 minutes.

10. Turn the oven down to 160°C (325°F/Gas 3) and cook for a further 3 hours, basting with a syringe baster every 30 minutes so that the cloth remains moist at all times.

11. One hour before the bird is ready, pour the orange and lemon juices over it and baste thoroughly as before. If the stuffed neck part of the bird seems to be drying out, protect it with a piece of foil.

12. At 1.30 pm the bird should be cooked – the juices should run clear if the fleshy part of the thigh is pricked with a skewer. Uncover the bird – it will be a rich mahogany brown – and discard the cloth. Lift it on to a carving dish, then cover loosely with foil and leave in a warm place for 30 minutes before carving.

13. To make the gravy, mix the cornflour (cornstarch) with the vermouth or sherry to a smooth cream.

14. Pour the fat from the roasting tin into a bowl, reserving the juices in the tin. To these add a cupful of the measured stock and put over a low heat, stirring well to release any brown bits sticking to the bottom of the tin.

15. Pour into a 20cm (8-inch) pan, bring to the boil and then add the remaining stock and the cornflour liquid.

16. Bring to the boil again, stirring well. Leave to simmer, uncovered, stirring occasionally, for a further 10 minutes until slightly thickened.

17. Taste and season with salt and black pepper.

Succulent Roast Turkey

Every year brings yet another 'foolproof' method for producing the perfect turkey. I learned of this method 30 years ago from an American magazine article, and I haven't yet been tempted to alter it. That's not to say that there are not many other successful ways.

This one is ideal for a large bird. However, for a small bird of 3.5–4kg (7–8 lb) the temperature can be higher and the cooking time much shorter. Preheat the oven to 230°C (450°F/Gas 8). Brush the bird all over with olive oil and set it on a rack in the roasting tin. Place in the oven, then immediately turn down to 190°C (375°F/Gas 5), allowing 20 minutes per 450g (1 lb). Thirty minutes before the bird is done, brush with 1 tablespoon each lemon juice and honey, then repeat once more 15 minutes before the end of the cooking time.

Turkey Helzel Stuffing

Sufficient to stuff the crop of a 4.5–7.2kg (10–16 lb) bird

215g (7½oz/scant 2 cups)
  plain (all-purpose) flour
40g (1½oz/scant ¼ cup) fine
  matzah meal
about 6 rounded tbsp raw
  chicken or turkey fat, cut
  or chopped into tiny
  pieces or 75g (3oz/⅓ cup)
  margarine, rendered
  chicken fat, or simulated
  chicken fat
1 tsp salt
good pinch of white pepper
1 large onion, finely grated

This makes a firm, savoury and easily sliced stuffing for the crop.

1. Mix all the ingredients together with a fork – the mixture should look uniformly moist, neither cloggy (it needs more flour), nor crumbly (add a little more fat).

2. Stuff the mixture loosely into the crop of the turkey – but be sure to push it well down so that the breast is plumped up nicely.

3. Sew the neck skin to the backbone.

Note: If neck skin is broken, arrange the helzel in a 'sausage' 4cm (1½″) in diameter on a piece of foil, then enclose and gently shape into a roll. Roast beside the turkey for 1½ hours.

Turkey Helzel Stuffing

To partner the robust flavours of turkey and all its trimmings, it takes a good pinch of imagination to transform mundane winter vegetables such as carrots and broccoli into dishes that are equally at home in a family meal or a dinner party menu.

Consider the mature carrots now in season. For 6 servings, first peel 675g (1?1/2 lb), then slice them thinly, but on the diagonal to make them look more interesting. Cook them in boiling salted water until tender. Drain well, then toss them in the same pan with a tablespoon each of runny honey and sesame seeds. Sprinkle with a little coarse sea salt and serve.

A minted carrot purée is another easy option. For 6–8 people, you'll need 900g (2 lb) boiled carrots, puréed in the food processor with 1 tsp freeze-dried mint, a generous tablespoon of butter (margerine for a meat meal), a teaspoon each of brown sugar and salt, and ?1/4 tsp white pepper.

Broccoli, a somewhat boring vegetable when plain boiled – is quite transformed by a touch of garlic and ginger. Divide 450g (1 lb) broccoli into little heads and boil until barely tender. Meanwhile, thinly slice two cloves of garlic and a 2.5cm (1-inch) piece of peeled fresh ginger and sauté in 3 tablespoons of olive oil until a pale gold – don't let the garlic brown or it will be bitter. Pour over the broccoli and serve.

Baked Chestnut Stuffing

Serves 10–12

Leftovers keep 3 days in the refrigerator. Freezes well, cooked or uncooked, for up to 3 months.

It's most convenient to bake this while the turkey is 'resting' out of the oven, before being carved. There are no eggs in this recipe, which results in a fluffier stuffing.

1. Drain the canned chestnuts, if used.

2. Melt the fat without colouring it, then simmer the chopped onion until soft and golden.

3. Meanwhile, coarsely chop the chestnuts and put in a bowl with the breadcrumbs, parsley and seasonings.

4. Pour on the fat and onions and mix well.

5. Preheat the oven to 190°C (375°F/Gas 5).

6. Spoon the stuffing into an ovenproof casserole. Bake, covered, for 20–25 minutes, until heated right through.

7. Serve from the casserole or spoon into a decorative serving dish.

2 x 425g (15oz) cans whole chestnuts or 2 x 200g packs of shrink-wrapped cooked chestnuts
150g (5oz/$\frac{2}{3}$ cup) melted margarine
1 large onion, peeled and finely chopped
225g (8oz/4 cups) fresh breadcrumbs
2 tbsp chopped parsley
2 tsp salt
$\frac{1}{4}$ tsp white pepper

Baked Chestnut Stuffing

The chestnut is one ingredient that is equally at home in either a savoury or a sweet dish. However, peeling fresh chestnuts is truly a labour of love, usually leading to sore fingers and a bad temper!

Fortunately, convenience has now entered the equation and you can buy canned chestnut purée, both sweetened and unsweetened, whole chestnuts in cans, and cooked whole chestnuts in shrink-wrap which keep fresh for months – all ready to use.

Without the chestnuts needing any preparation, stuffing for a turkey can be made in minutes. All you need to do is to sauté plenty of chopped onion in margarine, then combine it with the chestnuts and flavoured breadcrumbs.

75

Hanukkah Kibbeh

Serves 8

Keeps 3 days in the refrigerator. Freeze 2 months.

For the crust:
1 large onion, finely grated
675g (1½ lb) raw minced
    (ground) beef or lamb
350g (12oz/2 cups) fine bul-
    gur (cracked wheat)
½ tsp salt
10 grinds of black pepper
2 tbsp cold water

For the meat filling:
1 large onion, finely
    chopped
2 tbsp oil
450g (1 lb) raw minced
    (ground) beef or lamb
1 egg
2 tbsp water
1 tsp ground cinnamon
1 tsp salt
10 grinds of black pepper
50g (2oz/½ cup) pine ker-
    nels, toasted
75g (3oz/⅓ cup) margarine,
    melted

Hanukkah Kibbeh

The spicy meat filling, studded with toasted pine kernels,
is sandwiched between two
layers of the unique bulgur
and meat 'pastry'. The final
result is similar in taste and
texture to the classic torpedo-
shaped kibbehs.

A delicious Sephardi treat for Hanukkah. Serve hot or at room temperature, as a main dish or in smaller portions for cocktails.

1. To make the crust: mix the grated onion and meat, kneading until smooth.

2. Put the bulgur (cracked wheat) into a sieve and rinse with cold water. Squeeze out the moisture.

3. Add to the meat mixture with the salt, pepper and cold water. Mix to a very smooth paste.

4. To make the filling: sauté the chopped onion in the oil until golden, then add the meat and stir with a fork until the meat loses its redness and starts to turn brown.

5. Beat the egg with the water, then add to the meat mixture, together with the seasoning and the pine kernels. (To toast pine kernels, either toss them over moderate heat in an ungreased frying pan until golden, or microwave on 100 per cent power for 4 minutes, stirring twice.)

6. Preheat the oven to 200°C (400°F/Gas 6).

7. Grease a shallow baking tin measuring about 22.5 x 32.5 x 2.5cm (9 x 13 x 1″) and spread half the crust mixture smoothly on the bottom. Cover with the meat mixture and spread the remaining crust mixture on top.

8. Score the top crust into diamonds with the point of a sharp knife, then drizzle the melted margarine over the top.

9. Bake for 30 minutes until the top is brown and crisp.

Hanukkah Fruit Cake

Makes one 17–20cm (7–8 inch) diameter cake (photograph between pages 120 and 121)

Keeps 3 months in an airtight container.

An exceedingly well-flavoured semi-rich fruit cake, with a very moist texture. It can be made with an electric mixer or a large capacity (3–3.5 litre/5–6-pint/3–3½-quart) food processor. The stout gives it added richness of flavour. Perfect for a tea party.

1. Preheat the oven to 160°C (325°F/Gas 3). Grease a 17–20cm (7–8 inch) diameter tin, 7–5cm (3″) deep, and line the bottom and sides with silicone or wax paper.

2. Mix the flour, ground almonds, baking powder, and spice.

To mix in an electric mixer:
3. Cream the butter or margarine until it is like mayonnaise, then gradually beat in the sugar until the mixture is fluffy.

4. Add the orange and lemon rinds, then beat in the eggs a little at a time, alternating with a little of the sifted flour mixture to prevent curdling.

5. Add the remaining flour and dried fruit mixture alternately. Finally, stir in the 4 tablespoons of stout.

To mix in a food processor (this method is possible only in a large-capacity machine)
6. Process the eggs and sugar for 2 minutes until thickened and lighter in colour, scraping down the sides after 30 seconds.

7. Add the fat, 1 tablespoon at a time, processing constantly – the mixture should now be the consistency of mayonnaise.

8. Add the 4 tablespoons stout and the grated rinds, and process until evenly blended.

9. Spoon the flour mixture into the processor, then pulse it only until evenly blended, scraping the sides down once with a rubber spatula.

275g (10oz/2½ cups) plain (all-purpose) flour, sifted
50g (2oz/½ cup) ground almonds
½ level tsp baking powder
2 level tsp mixed sweet spice
225g (8oz/1 cup) butter or soft margarine, at room temperature
225g (8oz/1 cup) light Muscovado sugar
finely grated rind of 1 orange and 1 lemon
4 eggs, beaten to blend
4 tbsp stout (e.g. Guinness)

For the dried fruit mixture:
225g (8oz/1½ cups) raisins
225g (8oz/1½ cups) sultanas (white raisins)
125g (4oz/½ cup) glacé (candied) cherries, quartered
125g (4oz/1 cup) walnuts, chopped

To soak the cake:
8 tbsp stout (e.g. Guinness)

Hanukkah Fruit Cake
continued

10. Spoon in the dried fruit mixture and pulse only until evenly blended.

To bake and complete the cake:
11. Turn the mixture into the prepared tin, level off, then bake for 1 hour.

12. Turn the oven down to 150°C (300°F/Gas 2). Bake a 17cm (7-inch) cake for a further hour, or a 20cm (8-inch) cake for a further $1\frac{1}{2}$–$1\frac{3}{4}$ hours, or until the top springs back when gently touched with the finger, and a skewer comes out clean from the centre.

13. Take the cake out of the oven and put on a cooling rack.

14. When quite cold, take out of the tin and turn over so the base is uppermost. Put a plate underneath the rack, then prick the cake all over with a skewer and gradually spoon over the remaining 8 tablespoons of the stout.

15. Wrap in foil, then put in an airtight tin. Leave at least 10 days before eating.

Rugelach with Two Fillings

Makes 24–32 according to size (photograph between pages 120 and 121)

Keep 2 weeks in an airtight container in the refrigerator.

For the pastry:
225g (8oz/1 cup) unsalted butter
225g (8oz/1 cup) curd (low- or medium-fat) cheese
2 tbsp icing (powdered) sugar
225g (8oz/2 cups) self-raising flour (or plain (all-purpose) flour with 2 tsp baking powder

The raw pastry should be allowed to firm up in the refrigerator overnight, or for at least 2 hours.

For one filling, I used a luxury mixed fruit mixture which includes glacé (candied) pineapple, apricots and cherries as well as the usual currants, raisins and sultanas. For the other, the combination of jam and ground nuts proved delectable.

1. Preheat the oven to 200°C (400°F/Gas 6).

2. Have the butter the consistency of Plasticine – pliable but not spreadable. Work it together with the curd cheese and icing (powdered) sugar with either a wooden spoon or a mixer fitted with the 'K' beater. Gradually work in the flour until a dough is formed.

78

3. Knead lightly with the fingers until smooth, then wrap in foil and flatten into a 2.5cm (1-inch) thick disc. Refrigerate.

4. To make either filling, combine all the ingredients.

5. Divide the dough into 4 portions. On a floured board roll each portion into a 22.5cm (9") circle, about 3 mm ($\frac{1}{8}$") thick (use a pan lid as a guide). Cut each circle into 6–8 pie-shaped wedges (according to the size you fancy; do one as a trial).

6. For the fruit and nut filling: spread each piece of pastry thinly with apricot jam, then scatter evenly with the filling.

7. For the strawberry and almond filling: spread each piece of pastry with the filling.

8. With either filling, keep clear of the edges.

9. Using either filling, roll each wedge from the broad end to the point, then curve slightly to form a croissant shape.

10. Whisk the egg white until frothy, then paint evenly over the rugelach and sprinkle with a thin layer of granulated sugar.

11. Bake for 20 minutes or until a rich golden brown.

For the fruit and nut filling:
225g (8oz/1½ cups)
   luxury mixed dried fruit
small eating apple, grated
50g (2oz/¼ cup) chopped
   walnuts
   or pecans
1 tsp cinnamon
2 tbsp medium light
   Muscovado sugar
2 tbsp toasted coconut

To spread on pastry:
apricot jam

For the strawberry and almond filling:
4 rounded tbsp strawberry
   preserve mixed with
   4 rounded tbsp
   ground almonds

For the glaze:
1 egg white
granulated sugar

Rugelach

Say 'Hanukkah' today and everyone thinks of potato latkes. Yet that tradition cannot be more than 250 years old – the potato, now a staple food began to be widely cultivated in Europe only in the early part of the eighteenth century. Before that time the traditional foods of the Festival were mainly based on 'kaes' – the fresh white cheese that was a vital part of the diet in the Pale of Settlement. Cheese was chosen as a symbolic Hanukkah food because of its association with the tale, related in the Apocrypha, of the Hasmonean heroine Judith and the wine and cheese party she gave for Holofernes, the Greek General who ended up without his head!

Kaes was used to make fritters similar to latkes, or a wonderful cheese pastry. This pastry is flaky and crisp and very easy to roll out. It is made with only flour, butter and cheese – and no added liquid at all. (There is also a yeast-raised version mixed with sour cream.)

You can use it to make a delicious variation on dried fruit strudel, but the goodies that are particularly associated with this Festival are rugelach – which can best be described as sweet-filled croissants. Their origin is obscure – very few of my Jewish books include a recipe for them. One clue to their origin – the cook book published by the Lubavitch Women's Organization of the USA features a diagram showing how to shape them – so it is possible they originated in Poland. Certainly they are on the menu of most New York delis.

They need to be better known in Britain as they are extremely delicious – and quickly made. And once you've tried my version, you can experiment with any dried-fruit strudel filling.

Sufganiyot (Israeli-style Doughnuts)

Makes 24 doughnuts (photograph between pages 120 and 121)

Keep 2 days in the refrigerator. Freeze raw 1 month, cooked 3 months.

2 sachets of easy-blend
  (quick-rising) yeast
25g (1oz/2 tbsp) caster
  (superfine) sugar
450g (1 lb/4 cups) plain
  (all-purpose) flour
pinch of salt
300 ml (10 floz/1¼ cups)
  hand-hot milk
4 egg yolks
125g (4oz/½ cup) very soft
  butter
oil for frying
tart jam such as apricot or
  blackcurrant for filling
caster (superfine) sugar for
  coating

These doughnuts freeze extremely well and may be reheated either in a microwave or uncovered in a moderate oven. This particular version came my way from a Hungarian friend, and these sufganiyot are the most delicious I know.

1. Mix the yeast thoroughly with the sugar, flour and salt, then add the milk, egg yolks and butter to the bowl.

2. Beat everything together for 5 minutes, until the very soft dough looks smooth, shiny and elastic and leaves the sides of the bowl and the beater clean.

3. Leave in the bowl, covered with clingfilm (plastic wrap), and allow to rise until double in bulk – about 1½ hours.

4. Turn out on to a floured board and if the dough is at all sticky, work in a little more flour so that it is soft but easily rolled out.

5. Roll out to 1cm (⅜ inch) thick and cut into rounds about 5cm (2″) across.

6. Leave the rounds on the board, covered with a tea (dish) towel, and let them rise until puffy – about 20 minutes.

7. Have the deep-fryer heated to 185°C (365°F) – it should not be quite as hot as for fried fish.

8. Fry the doughnuts in batches until a rich brown on both sides, leaving room for them to swell. Then lift out and drain well.

9. Make a little slit in each doughnut and insert a teaspoonful of the jam, then roll in the caster sugar.

Ginger & Citrus Shortbread Fingers

Makes approximately 22

Keep 2 weeks in an airtight container. Freeze 3 months.

A superb variation of shortbread, with the added delight of ginger. These are ideal for a Hanukkah tea party.

1. Preheat the oven to 190°C, (375°F/Gas 5). Have ready an ungreased tin measuring 30 x 20cm (12 x 8") by 2.5cm (1") deep.

Using a food processor:
2. Put all the ingredients (except the ginger) into the food processor and pulse until they are just beginning to cling together in tiny lumps.

3. Tip into a bowl and stir in the chopped ginger, then gather the mixture together and knead into a soft dough.

By hand:
4. Rub the butter (cut into 2.5cm/1-inch chunks) into the dry ingredients until the mixture is beginning to cling together in tiny lumps. Then stir in the ginger, rinds, and egg yolks and knead to a smooth dough.

Using either method:
5. Press the dough into the tin in an even layer, then press down with a slightly smaller tin. Prick all over with a fork or skewer.

6.. Bake for 10 minutes, then turn the oven down to 160°C, (325°F/Gas 3) and bake for a further 25–30 minutes until the shortbread is a pale gold in colour.

7. Put the tin on a cooling tray for 10 minutes, then sprinkle lightly with caster sugar and cut into fingers approximately 5 x 2.5cm (2 x 1").

8. Remove from the tin, and when quite cold, store in an airtight container.

275g (10oz/2½ cups) plain (all-purpose) flour
50g (2oz/½ cup) cornflour (cornstarch)
125g (4oz/½ cup) golden caster (superfine) sugar
225g (8oz/1 cup) butter, cut in approx. 2.5cm (1-inch) chunks
2 egg yolks
grated rind of 1 orange and 1 lemon
125g (4oz/½ cup) crystallized (candied) ginger, roughly chopped, or stem ginger, washed, dried and chopped

Rich Steamed Hanukkah Pudding with Dried Fruits

Serves 10–12.

Makes 1 x 17.5-20cm (7–8 inch) diameter pudding. Keeps in a cool cupboard at least 1 year.

125g (4oz/¾ cup) stoned (pitted) and tenderised prunes
125g (4oz/¾ cup)
dried dates
450 g(1 lb/2 cups) luxury
mixed dried fruit
150 ml (5 floz/⅔ cup)
Guinness or other stout or
ale
75g (3oz/¾ cup) self-raising
flour (or plain (all-pur-
pose) flour with scant tsp
baking powder)
scant tsp salt
¾ level tsp each
ground nutmeg,
ground cinnamon
and ground mixed spice
finely grated rind of 1 orange
and 1 lemon
50g (2oz/½ cup)
ground almonds
225g (8oz/1 cup) white cooking fat or margarine
175g (6oz/3 cups) fine fresh
breadcrumbs
175g (6oz/¾ cup)
soft brown sugar
4 large eggs

To pour over when cold:
3 tbsp brandy or rum

A little goes a long way!

1. Chop the prunes and dates finely and put in a bowl with the mixed dried fruit. Pour over the Guinness or ale.

2. Cover with clingfilm (plastic wrap) and cook on 100 per cent power in the microwave for 4 minutes. Then allow to stand, covered, until cold.

3. When ready to mix the pudding, put the flour, salt, spices, grated rinds, ground almonds, white fat, breadcrumbs and sugar into a very large mixing bowl. Add the soaked fruits and mix very thoroughly.

4. Whisk the eggs until slightly thickened, then add to the mixture and stir well. Spoon into a greased pudding basin and cover first with silicone paper and then with foil.

5. Refrigerate overnight or for several hours.

6. Steam for 6 hours, or put in a pan two-thirds full of boiling water and boil for the same time, topping up with more boil-ing water from the kettle from time to time.

7. Remove from the heat and allow to cool. Uncover then spoon over the brandy or rum. Cover with fresh silicone paper and foil and store in a cool place.

8. On the day, steam or boil for a further 4 hours. Serve with the Sherry Sauce (p. 83).

Steamed Hanukkah Pudding

A pudding with a definite Anglo-Jewish flavour – the prunes, dates and stout suggest it could well be of Victorian or Edwardian origin. The length of time given for steaming is not a printer's error – it ensures that, even if you make the pudding only the week before, it will still be dark and juicy on the day.

Foaming Sherry Sauce

Serves 8.

Use immediately after making, or make just before the meal and then leave over hot (not boiling) water and whisk again just before serving.

1. Put the egg yolks and sugar into a heat-proof basin or the top of a double saucepan and whisk until pale and mousse-like (quickest with a hand-held electric whisk.)

2. Whisk in the cornflour (cornstarch) and sherry.

3. Stand the basin (or pan) over a pan of simmering water and whisk constantly until the mixture becomes thick and foamy, about 3-4 minutes.

4. Serve with the Steamed Hanukkah Pudding (p. 82).

3 egg yolks
75g (3oz/⅓ cup)
   caster (superfine) sugar
1½ tsp cornflour
   (cornstarch)
150ml (5 floz/⅔ cup) medium (Amontillado) sherry

Foaming Sherry Sauce

This fluffy sauce is first cousin to both the German 'weinchadeau' and the Italian 'zabaglione'. It is a perfect partner to the rich Hanukkah Pudding in any language. To enjoy it at its best, divide the preparation in two: before the meal, whisk together the egg yolks and sugar as described in (1.) Then when the main course has been finished, complete as described in (2.) and (3.).

Easy Parev Ice-Cream

Makes 3 litres (5 pints/3 quarts).

Freezes 1 month

6 large eggs
1 x 500g (18oz) carton (2 cups)
 parev whipping cream
200g (7oz/scant 1 cup) caster
 (superfine) sugar
1 tsp vanilla extract

This recipe does need a Kenwood or other large mixer to handle the volume. Leave at room temperature for 20 minutes to soften before serving.

Note: This recipe contains uncooked eggs.

1. Put the eggs, parev cream, sugar and vanilla extract in the mixer bowl. Whisk at high speed until the mixture has the texture of whipped cream, this will take about 5 minutes and the mixture will then almost fill the bowl.

2. The mixture can be frozen in one large carton or divided into two and each half flavoured with any of the following, added just before freezing:

      225g (8oz) strawberries, chopped;
  or 1 tsp ground cinnamon;
  or 125g (4oz) chocolate mints, chopped;
  or 175g (6oz) chopped canned chestnuts;
  or 100g (3!soz) pack chocolate drops (morsels).

Parev Ice-Cream

I came home from a recent visit to London bearing a long sought-after trophy – a simple but scrumptious recipe for parev ice-cream.

Unlike many ice-creams made without an ice-cream maker, this one achieves a beautiful texture without any beating of egg whites or stirring half way – you simply put all the ingredients in a bowl and leave the mixer to do the rest. The result? Nearly 3 litres (5 pints/3quarts) of 'creamy' parev ice-cream, whose flavour – with a little imagination – can be varied almost infinitely.

Such a quantity made in 5 minutes undoubtedly makes this recipe the winner as regards preparation time, and if you have some non-dairy cream in the freezer, you don't even need to go out of the house for the ingredients.

The home-made version certainly scores on price as against commercial parev ice cream, but not so much that this counts as the main reason for making it. But you are in complete control of everything that goes into the ice-cream.

Hot Spiced Wine Cup

Serves 12, 2 x 125-ml (4-floz) glasses per person

A wonderful way to get a Hanukkah party going!

1. The day before serving, put all the ingredients (except the sugar and the liqueur) into an enamelled or stainless steel pan and mix thoroughly. Cover and leave overnight.

2. An hour before using, add the sugar and liqueur and bring slowly to the boil, then immediately turn the heat down so that it is barely bubbling.

3. Taste and add more sugar if required. Leave at steaming point until served.

2 litres (3 bottles)
  any red wine
300 ml (10 floz/1¼ cups)
  water
1 tbsp Angostura Bitters,
  if available
6 whole cardamom pods,
  slightly crushed (with
  the end of a rolling pin)
6 whole cloves
2.5cm (1-inch) piece peeled
  fresh ginger
1 cinnamon stick
¼ tsp ground nutmeg
125–175g (4–6oz) sugar
  (depending on acidity
  of wine)
4 tbsp Cointreau or other
  orange-flavoured liqueur

Purim
The Feast of Lots

Purim is very much a light-hearted folk Festival: there's a beautiful Jewish Queen, Esther; a rebellious Queen, Vashti; a villain, Haman; and a hero, Mordecai. And in the middle of the story, the mighty King Ahasuerus, Ruler of the Medes and Persians, whose empire extended from Ethiopia to India.

The villain Haman plotted to organize his own 'Final Solution' by destroying the entire Jewish population of Persia and pocketing all their riches. He cast lots to find out what would be the most propitious day – hence the name of the Festival. But by the intervention of Queen Esther, advised by her uncle, Mordecai, the head of the Jewish community, the plot was uncovered and Haman ended up on the gallows he had prepared for Mordecai.

So there is plenty of scope for pageantry and jollification in this story; children dress up to represent the main characters and act out the Purim story or 'Purim spiel' for the delight of their parents. Their elders follow the advice given by Mordecai to the Jewish community of the time that there should be a 'day of feasting and gladness and of sending portions one to another and gifts to the poor'. This advice is contained in a special scroll the 'Megillath Esther', which is read out in the synagogue on this one day of the year, mention of the Haman's name being a signal for all the children to make a noise with their 'dreiers' or 'greigers' (rattles).

To celebrate Purim, every Jewish community has its own customs, particularly when it comes to food. For example, in Ashkenazi households, the poppy seed symbolizes the Jewish gold with which Haman planned to fill his pockets; in Sephardi households it's often represented by sesame seeds.

One place where the two strands of symbolic foods intertwine is the Rue des Rosiers, a Parisian street of almost wholly Jewish shops and restaurants. Just before Purim, the seductive smell of poppy seeds is heavy on the air; in the windows of Florence Finkelsztain's bakery, which celebrates Gastronomie Yiddish, Europe, Centrale et Russes, the sachertorten and apfel strudels give pride of place to the 'houmentaschen', 'strudel pavot' and 'pain pavot' – the latter on crisp flat bread scattered with poppy seeds, quite different from the yard-long speciality of Polish Jews, the plaited 'kalischbrod' (Purim bread).

On the other side of the street stand the Glatt Kosher Yahalom Traiteur and its neighbour Le Roi de Felafel, offering chick peas and sesame seeds galore along with the caviar d'aubergine and salade Turque. For while poppy seed ('pavot' in French) spells Purim to European Jews, many Sephardim eat chick peas at this Festival to honour Queen Esther. As their tradition has it, she ate only vegetarian food at the court of her non-Jewish husband, King Ahasuerus, in order not to break the laws of Kashrut.

Back now to the present and to the custom, advised by Mordecai, of 'sending portions' – shalach manot – perhaps the most charming of the Purim customs, and common to both the Sephardi and the Ashkenazi communities. Often these 'portions of food' are in the form of fruit and chocolates, but the most welcome is surely a gift of home-baked goodies, particularly for the elderly whose baking days are over.

Most of the sweet things of Purim are three-cornered, whether that shape refers to Haman's pocket or his ears! This shape is found in the Hamantaschen, which are either made in the traditional way with yeast (see the soured cream ones on p. 92), or with pastry (see the prune ones on p. 10). Even the biscuits have three corners, whether they be in melt-in-the mouth Ras Tahini (irresistible with toasted sesame seeds), or the American Poppy Seed Treats. There's a recipe, too, for a strudel filled with poppy seeds or 'mohn' I saw in the Rue des Rosiers. A contemporary note is struck by a plaited loaf, with each strand filled with Parmesan and poppy seeds. For a savoury change in honour of Queen Esther, there's a wonderful salad, crunchy with nuts, rice and sesame seeds, and also delicious Turkey Schnitzels which are a new tradition in Israel today.

Purim Turkey Schnitzels

Serves 6–8

Serve hot off the pan.

6–8 ready-cut turkey
  schnitzels, each
  150–175g (5–6oz)
2 tbsp lemon juice
1 tsp salt
15 grinds of black pepper

For the coating:
1 heaped tbsp plain
  (all-purpose) flour
2 eggs beaten to blend with
  1 tbsp cold water
75g (3oz/¾ cup) each
  medium matzah meal
  and fine matzah meal (or
  175g (6oz/1½ cups) fine
  dry breadcrumbs)
½ tsp salt
15 grinds of black pepper
good pinch of paprika

For frying:
6 tbsp groundnut (peanut),
  or sunflower (canola) or
  olive oil

For garnish:
wedges of lime or lemon
sprigs of parsley

A variation on Wiener Schnitzels, which has become almost traditional on Israeli tables at Purim. Frying in groundnut oil ensures a crisp golden brown coating.

1. Lay each schnitzel between 2 pieces of greaseproof (wax) paper and pound with a cutlet bat or the end of a rolling pin until half the original thickness.

2. Put the lemon juice, salt and pepper into a shallow dish. Turn each slice in it to coat on both sides, then leave in the dish for 30 minutes, turning once.

3. Meanwhile, put the flour, eggs beaten with water, and matzah meal or dry crumbs, mixed with the seasonings, into 3 separate shallow dishes placed side by side. Dip each slice in the flour, patting off any excess with the hands. Brush with a thin layer of beaten egg and water, then turn in the seasoned matzah meal or crumbs, patting the coating on firmly.

4. Leave the schnitzels side by side on a board for 30 minutes to set the coating (longer will do no harm, but do refrigerate them).

5. In a large heavy frying pan, heat the oil until you can feel it comfortably warm on your hand held 5cm (2″) above the surface. Put in the schnitzels (don't crowd the pan) and cook them steadily for 5 minutes on each side, or until crisp and brown.

6. When they are cooked, lay them side by side on a baking tray in a slow oven, 140°C (275°F/Gas 1), to keep hot without drying out.

7. Serve garnished with the wedges of lime or lemon and the parsley.

Crunchy Brown Rice Salad

Serves 6–8

Keeps 2 days in the refrigerator. Do not freeze.

A superb salad with a gloriously crunchy texture. And it's positively bursting with nutritional goodies!

1. Put all the ingredients for the dressing into a screw-top jar and shake well to blend – about 1 minute.

2. Rinse the rice in a sieve to remove excess starch, then cook in boiling salted water for 30 minutes, or until bite-tender. Rinse and drain well.

3. To toast the nuts and seeds, spread the nuts to one side of a baking tray and the seeds to the other. Leave in a moderate oven, 180°C (350°F/Gas 4), until a rich brown, stirring every few minutes (the nuts will brown before the seeds and should be removed). Leave to cool.

4. Transfer the rice to a bowl while still warm and stir in the dressing. An hour before serving, add all the remaining ingredients. Toss thoroughly and transfer to a serving dish.

175g (6oz/1 cup) brown rice
½ tsp salt
50g (2oz/½ cup) toasted cashew nuts
2 tbsp toasted sunflower seeds
4 tbsp toasted sesame seeds
3 tbsp chopped parsley
1 x 325g (11½oz) can sweetcorn, drained
6 spring onions (green onions), plus 10cm (4″) of the green, finely sliced
1 each red, green and yellow peppers (bell peppers), cored, seeded and diced
50g (2oz/¼ cup) currants

For the dressing:
25 ml (1 floz/2 tbsp) sunflower (canola) oil
6 tbsp soy sauce
2 tbsp lemon juice
1 large clove of garlic, crushed
good pinch of sea salt
8 grinds of black pepper
1 tbsp peeled and finely chopped fresh ginger
1 seeded and finely chopped green (hot) chili pepper (optional)

Crunchy Brown Rice Salad

You no longer have to be a gardener to use herbs with a lavish hand. Just go to the supermarket and, for the same price as those minuscule packs, you can buy a whole plant – the majority grown in Britain.

You get more flavouring from fresh herbs in hot dishes if you add them shortly before serving. In cold ones, such as salad dressings, they can be added with the rest of the ingredients. The exception is basil, whose flavouring oil is particularly volatile. So tear (don't chop) the leaves – and add just before serving.

Hamantaschen with a Prune-and-Walnut Filling

Dried Fruit and Wine Filling

Makes 22–24   (photograph between pages 120 and 121)

Keep 4 days in an airtight container. Freeze 3 months.

For the pastry:
150g (5oz/⅔ cup) firm butter or block margarine
125g (4oz/1 cup) each plain
(all-purpose) and self-
raising flour or plain (all-
purpose) flour with 1 tsp
baking powder
50g (2oz/¼ cup) caster
(superfine) sugar
2 tsp grated lemon rind
1 beaten egg

For the prune-and-walnut
filling:
50g (2oz/⅓ cup) walnuts
1 x 250g (9oz) pack ready-
to-eat prunes
2 tsp lemon juice
2 rounded tbsp damson or
plum jam ('povidl')

A meltingly tender rich shortcrust pastry with a choice of juicy fillings.

1. Cut the fat into roughly 2.5cm (1″) chunks, then put in a food processor with the flour, baking powder (if used), caster sugar and lemon rind. Pulse 10 times to rub in the fat, then add the beaten egg and pulse until the mixture is beginning to cling together in little moist balls.

2. Tip out into a bowl, gather into a ball with the fingers and then, with lightly floured hands, knead gently until smooth. Pat into a disc about 2.5cm (1″) thick. Wrap in foil and refrigerate for several hours or overnight.

3. To make the prune-and-walnut filling, process the walnuts on the food processor until powdered. Then add the prunes, lemon juice and jam and pulse until it becomes a paste. Turn into a bowl and chill with the pastry.

4. To make the dried-fruit and-wine filling, combine all the ingredients in the order given. Turn into a bowl and leave at room temperature to mature until the pastry has chilled suf-ficiently.

5. Preheat the oven to 190°C (375°F/Gas 5).

6. Take the pastry from the refrigerator and if too firm for rolling, work a little with the hands to soften it (you may find it easier to divide the dough in half for rolling). Roll out 5 mm/(¼ inch) thick on a board sprinkled lightly with icing (powdered) sugar.

7. Cut into rounds with a 7.5cm (3-inch) plain cutter and put a rounded teaspoonful of filling in the centre of each circle. Draw up to form a tricorne (three-cornered) pastry, leaving a little gap in the centre to allow steam to escape. Brush lightly with the glaze and sprinkle with the sugar.

8. Arrange on ungreased baking trays and bake for 15 minutes until golden brown.

9. Store when cold in an airtight container. Sprinkle with icing (powdered) sugar (if used) just before serving.

Hamantaschen with a Prune-and-Walnut or Dried-Fruit-&-Wine Filling

I was very cheered recently to get a resounding 'Yes!' when I asked a student audience, 'Do you intend to eat traditional Jewish foods when you have your own home?' However, in reply to the question, 'And do you intend to cook them yourselves?', a hush fell over the group – a response that surely reflects the situation in the general community, where everyone talks and reads about food, yet home cooking is falling out of favour.

So what's the future for that archetypal Purim treat, the Hamantasch? (The word is the Yiddish version of the German 'mohntasch', a pocket of dough filled with poppy seeds which was popular in the early Middle Ages.) By tradition, it's made with a time-consuming yeast dough – an easy option in years gone by when this dough was made every week in most Jewish homes for challot and kuchen. Today I guess that only a few intrepid souls follow this custom and at least 95 per cent of yeasty Hamantaschen are bought at the baker's. I find nothing wrong with that. After all, it is the triangular shape of Hamantaschen, rather than the actual dough used, that is the important thing. All that is needed to continue the home-made tradition is to substitute a pastry more in keeping with today's – and tomorrow's – lifestyle.

The ones made with a 'muerbeteig' pastry – a rich shortcrust, sweetened with just a little icing (powered) sugar – are easy to make. This particular one is lovely and short and the resulting goodies really do melt in the mouth.

Neither of the fillings for the Hamantaschen contain the traditional poppy seeds, because unless you can buy them ready-ground they can be gritty. However, grinding is easy if you have an electric coffee- or nut-mill.

Be warned though! Although a small glass of wine helps the baking session along, don't take too literally the religious injunction to drink so much that you cannot distinguish between the hero Mordecai and the villain Haman!

For the dried-fruit-and-wine filling:
350g (12oz/2 cups) mixed dried fruit
1 small apple, finely grated
50g (2oz/$\frac{1}{3}$ cup) walnuts, coarsely chopped
25g (1oz/2 tbsp) soft brown sugar
1 tbsp ginger marmalade or honey
1 tbsp warm golden (corn) syrup
$\frac{1}{2}$ tsp cinnamon
$\frac{1}{2}$ tsp mixed spice
pinch of ground nutmeg
grated rind and juice of half a lemon
1 tbsp brandy (optional)
1 tbsp sweet kiddush (port-type) wine
40g (1$\frac{1}{2}$oz/3 tbsp) melted butter or margarine

For the glaze:
1 egg yolk mixed with 2 tsp cold water
golden granulated sugar

For sprinkling on top:
icing (powdered) sugar – optional

Soured Cream Hamantaschen

Makes 8 large Hamantaschen

Keep 3 days in the refrigerator. Freeze 3 months.

For the dough:
2 x 6–7g (¼oz) sachets easy-blend (quick-rising) dried yeast
500g (1lb 2oz/4½ cups) plain strong bread flour
1 level tsp salt
125g (4oz/½ cup) caster (superfine) sugar
125 ml (4 floz/½ cup) luke-warm milk
2 eggs
75g (3oz/⅓ cup) melted butter
150 ml (5 floz/⅔ cup) soured cream

For the poppy-seed filling:
125g (4oz/1 cup) poppy seeds, ready-ground if available
125 ml (4 floz/½ cup) milk
25g (1oz/2 tbsp) butter
50g (2oz/¼ cup) caster (superfine) sugar
2 level tbsp golden (corn) syrup
50g (2oz/⅓ cup) seedless raisins, chopped
50g (2oz/½ cup) walnuts, chopped
½ tsp vanilla extract
½ tsp grated lemon rind

For the glaze:
honey or golden (corn) syrup

These provide a totally different taste experience from the baker's yeast Hamantaschen. A friend to whom I served them went misty-eyed because of their similarity to her Viennese grandmother's baking.

1. In a large bowl, mix the easy-blend dried yeast with the dry ingredients.

2. Make a well in the centre and drop in the milk, eggs, melted butter and soured cream.

3. Gradually stir in the surrounding flour and beat either with the 'K' beater or a wooden spoon (or, as I prefer, with the hand in a fine surgical glove) until a soft dough is formed. Keep on beating until the dough leaves the beater or the fingers clean – about 5 minutes. Add an extra tablespoon or two of flour if the dough is still sticky.

4. Grease the inside of a plastic bag with a few drops of oil (the bag should be big enough to allow the dough to expand). Tip the mixture into the bag, close loosely and refrigerate overnight.

5. Next day, divide the dough into 8 even pieces about 125g/4oz each (13–15cm/5–6″) – you can weigh them to make sure. Then knead each into a ball and roll out into a circle 13-15cm (5-6″) in diameter.

6. Meanwhile, make the filling by grinding the poppy seeds if necessary in a coffee- or nut-mill. Then put in a small pan and stir in the milk, followed by all the other ingredients (except the vanilla and lemon rind), and cook until thick – about 5 minutes – stirring constantly. Add the vanilla and lemon rind when cold.

7. Spread a tablespoonful of filling in the middle of each of the 8 dough pieces and draw the edges together to make a three-cornered shape (see opposite).

8. Arrange the Hamantaschen on greased baking sheets, leaving room between to allow for expansion. Place the tray(s) in a large plastic bag, and leave in a warm place until double in bulk – about 1 hour. At this stage the Hamantaschen will look puffy and feel spongy when gently pressed with the finger.

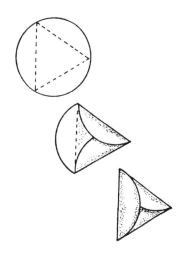

9. Preheat the oven to 190°C (375°F/Gas 5) and bake the Hamantaschen for 25 minutes or until a rich brown.

10. Have ready a little liquid honey or warm golden syrup. Brush on top of the Hamantaschen as they come out of the oven.

11. To serve, slice diagonally like strudel and serve plain or lightly buttered.

Cheese Filling for Hamantaschen (Variation)

Makes 8 large Hamantaschen

Keep 3 days in the refrigerator. Freeze 3 months.

1. Put the cheese into a bowl, then beat in all the remaining ingredients. The mixture should be the consistency of butter icing (frosting). If it is too dry, add a little yoghurt or milk.

2. Chill while the Hamantaschen dough is rising.

3. Continue from Step 7.

375g (12oz/1½ cups) curd (low- or medium-fat) cheese
50g (2oz/¼ cup) caster (superfine) sugar
grated rind of half a lemon
½ tsp vanilla extract
2 tsp custard powder (vanilla pudding mix) or cornflour (cornstarch)
50g (2oz/⅓ cup) sultanas (white raisins)

Sephardi Purim Date Pastries

Makes 20–22

Keep 1 week at room temperature in an airtight container. Freeze 3 months.

For the pastry:
125g (4oz/1 cup) plain (all-purpose) flour and 125g (4oz/1 cup) self-raising flour (or 225g (8oz/2 cups) plain (all-purpose) flour with 1 level tsp baking powder)
40g (1½oz/3 tbsp) caster (superfine) sugar
150g (5oz/⅔ cup) butter or chilled margarine
1 large egg

For the filling:
250g (9oz/generous 1½ cups) stoned (pitted) dates
125 ml (4 floz/½ cup) water
25g (1oz/2 tbsp) butter or margarine
1 tsp cinnamon
squeeze of lemon juice

Icing (powdered) sugar for sprinkling on top after baking

The method of making these delicious morsels was taught to me by a lady who was born in Damascus, Syria. It resembles the Ashkenazi way of preparing a strudel, with a sweetened dough enclosing the date filling.

1. Make the pastry by the rubbing-in method or in a food processor as follows. Into the bowl put the dry ingredients and the well-chilled fat cut into roughly 2.5cm (1-inch) chunks.

2. Whisk the egg to blend, then turn on the machine and pour the egg down the feed tube, pulsing only until the mixture begins to form little damp balls. Then tip it into a bowl and gather together into a dough.

3. With either method, turn the pastry on to a board or counter-top sprinkled with a very light layer of flour. Knead it gently with the fingertips to remove any cracks, then flatten into a 2.5cm (1-inch) thick disc. Wrap in foil or clingfilm (plastic wrap), then chill for 30 minutes.

4. To make the filling: cut up the dates with scissors. If very hard, put in a small bowl with 50 ml (2 floz/¼ cup) water, then cover and heat on 100 per cent power in a microwave for 2 minutes. The water will now be absorbed. Put in a small pan together with the remaining water.

5. If not using a microwave, put the cut-up dates into a small pan with the 125 ml (4 floz/½ cup) water.

6. In either case, add the butter or margarine and cook over gentle heat, stirring until the mixture becomes a smooth, spreadable paste. Stir in the cinnamon and lemon juice. Allow to cool.

7. Preheat the oven to 180°C (350°F/Gas 4).

8. Divide the dough into two even balls and roll each one
   on a floured board into a rectangle measuring approximately
   30 x 20cm (12 x 8˝).

9. Spread each rectangle of pastry with half the date mixture,
   leaving 1.25cm (½ inch) of pastry clear all round the edges.
   Turn in the edges of the shorter sides to enclose the filling,
   then roll the pastry over twice as for a flat strudel.

10. Lift carefully on to an ungreased tray, with the join
    underneath and leaving 5cm (2˝) between each roll. Prick all
    over with a fork (to stop the pastry bursting),
    then bake for 20 minutes until the top is firm and a
    pale gold.

11. Cool for 10 minutes on the baking tray, then carefully trans-
    fer to a wire cooling tray. When at room temperature, lift on
    to a board and sprinkle thickly with icing (powdered) sugar.
    Cut diagonally into slices about 2.5cm (1 inch) wide. Store
    in an airtight container.

Purim Date Pastries

One of the glories of
Sephardi Purim baking is a
date-filled pastry called vari-
ously 'mamoule', 'klaitcha',
'ras ib adivah' or 'menenas',
depending on whether the
recipe comes with an
Egyptian, Iranian or Syrian
accent.

Like many Sephardi recipes,
the 'mamoule' are labour-
intensive – making them in the
traditional way involves
moulding little cups of pastry
with your fingers, adding a
date filling, then sealing and
decorating the top either using
special little tweezers or a
wooden mould called a 'tabi'.

If you're thinking at this
point that making these pastries is not for you, there is a
simpler way which is equally
delicious – so please read my
recipe before you make up
your mind!

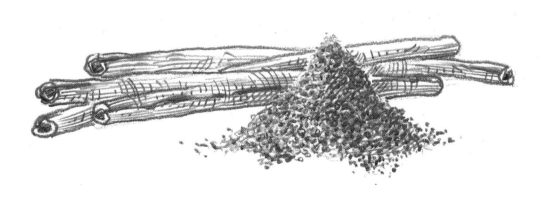

Purim Poppy-Seed Treats

Makes about 30

Keeps 1 week in an airtight container. Freeze 2 months.

50g (2oz/$\frac{1}{4}$ cup) butter or
firm margarine
50g (2oz/$\frac{1}{4}$ cup) caster
(superfine) sugar
2 egg yolks
1 tsp vanilla extract
175g (6oz/1$\frac{1}{2}$ cups) self-raising flour (or plain (all-
purpose) flour with 1$\frac{1}{2}$
level tsp baking powder)

For the topping:
2 egg whites
pinch of cream of tartar
125g (4oz/$\frac{1}{2}$ cup) medium
brown sugar
150g (5oz/1$\frac{1}{4}$ cups) poppy
seeds, ground

Purim Poppy-Seed Treats

For the Poppy-Seed Treats, it's important to use ground seeds. The days are long gone when anyone had the time to crush poppy seeds by hand; now a coffee or food mill, perhaps powered by an electric mixer such as a Kenwood does the job in seconds. And sometimes you can buy the seeds ready-ground.

An American interpretation of the Hamantaschen – a rich, buttery base is topped with a brown sugar meringue crammed with poppy seeds and cut into triangles.

1. Preheat the oven to 180°C (350°F/Gas 4).

2. Put the butter or margarine, cut into 2.5cm (1-inch) chunks, the caster sugar, egg yolks, vanilla and flour into the food processor and process until like moist crumbs. Then press firmly into a greased tin measuring approximately 17 x 28 x 5cm (7 x 11 x 2").

3. Whisk the egg whites with the cream of tartar until they form soft peaks, then gradually beat in the brown sugar until firm peaks are formed.

4. Fold in the poppy seeds, then spread the meringue evenly over the pastry base.

5. Bake for 30 minutes until the surface is firm to the touch and lightly browned, then cut into approximately thirty 4cm (1$\frac{1}{2}$-inch) triangles.

Ras Tahini (Moroccan Sesame Triangles)

Makes 30–36 (photograph between pages 120 and 121)

Keep for up to a month in an airtight container. Freeze 3 months.

The toasted sesame seeds impart a bewitching flavour to these crisp yet tender biscuits from the Sephardi cuisine.

1. Preheat the oven to 190°C (375°F/Gas 5). Have ready two ungreased baking sheets.

2. To toast the sesame seeds, heat a small dry (preferably non-stick) frying pan for 3 minutes, then add the seeds and toast them until golden brown – keep shaking the pan and watch them carefully as they burn easily.

3. In a food processor, process the fat, sugar, vanilla and flour until the mixture begins to form little moist balls, then add the sesame seeds and pulse for 4 seconds.

4. Tip on to a board and knead gently to form a smooth 'plastic' dough. Chill for 1 hour.

5. Roll the dough 5 mm ($\frac{1}{4}$ inch) thick on a floured board, then cut into 3cm ($1\frac{1}{4}$ inch) triangles.

6. Place 1.25cm ($\frac{1}{2}$ inch) apart on the baking sheets. Bake for 10–11 minutes until golden brown. Take from the oven and sprinkle with caster (superfine) sugar.

7. Store at room temperature in an airtight container.

50g (2oz/$\frac{1}{2}$ cup) sesame seeds, toasted until golden

175g (6oz/$\frac{3}{4}$ cup) butter or block margarine

50g (2oz/$\frac{1}{3}$ cup) icing (powdered) sugar

$\frac{1}{2}$ tsp vanilla extract

225g (8oz/2 cups) self-raising flour (or plain (all-purpose) flour with 2 level tsp baking powder)

For decoration:
caster (superfine) sugar

Russian Mohn Torte (Poppy Seed Cake)

Makes 1 x 22.5cm (9-inch) ring cake

Keeps 4 days in an airtight container. Freeze 3 months.

2 eggs
225g (8oz/1 cup) caster
  (superfine) sugar
1 tsp vanilla extract
175g (6oz/1½ cups) ground poppy
  seeds
2 tsp finely grated orange rind
125g (4oz/1 cup) sponge self-raising flour (or plain (all-purpose) flour with 1 level tsp
  baking powder)
125 ml (4 floz/½ cup) milk
125g (4oz/½ cup) unsalted butter,
  melted and cooled
2 tbsp sunflower (canola) oil

For greasing the tin:
sunflower (canola) oil

To dust the cake:
icing (powdered) sugar

This cake from nineteenth-century Eastern Europe is now a staple of American coffee shops! It has the fine, delicate, moist texture of a Genoese sponge.

1. Preheat the oven to 180°C (350°F/Gas 4). Carefully oil a 22.5cm (9-inch) ring tin or use a non-stick one.

2. With an electric whisk, beat the eggs, sugar, and vanilla for 4–5 minutes, until the mixture lightens in colour and is almost as thick as softly whipped cream. Stir in the poppy seeds and orange rind. Gently fold in the sifted flour alternately with the milk, followed by the cooled butter and the oil.

3. Spoon into the prepared tin and bake for 40–45 minutes, until the surface is firm to a gentle touch.

4. Leave the cake in the tin on a cooling tray for 10 minutes, then run a knife around the edges of the tin and turn it out on to the cooling tray. When it is quite cold, dust it thickly with icing sugar.

Hungarian Mohn Strudel (Poppyseed Strudel)

Makes 3 strudels, each about 30cm (12″) long

Keep 4 days in the refrigerator. Freeze 3 months.

This exquisite strudel from the former Austro-Hungarian Empire is one of the finest yeast cakes I know. Natural poppy seeds can be used, but ground ones give the strudel a smoother texture in the mouth.

1. The dough is best made with the 'K' beater of a Kenwood or a wooden spoon, as it is too soft for a dough hook.

2. Mix the yeast in the bowl with the flour, caster sugar and salt, then add all the remaining ingredients.

3. Now beat until the dough is smooth and stretchy and can be pulled away from the beater, leaving it almost clean. This will take about 5 minutes. If the dough is still a little sticky, don't be afraid to work in a tablespoon or two of plain (all-purpose) flour. (I beat the dough with one hand, wearing a fine surgical glove.)

4. Tip the dough out of the bowl. Grease the bowl with oil, then put the dough back in and turn it over so that it is lightly coated with the oil. Cover the bowl with clingfilm (plastic wrap) and leave in a warm kitchen until it has doubled in volume ($1\frac{1}{4}$–$1\frac{1}{2}$ hours).

5. Meanwhile, make the filling. If the poppy seeds are whole, grind them in a nut- or coffee-mill until they are like ground almonds, then put them in a pan with all the remaining ingredients. Bring to the boil, stirring, then bubble for 5 minutes until the filling is thick but still juicy. Allow to go cold.

6. To assemble the strudel: tip the risen dough on to a floured board and knead with the hands for 2 minutes. Then divide into three equal pieces weighing 225g (8oz) each. Knead each piece into a ball.

7. Roll out each piece of dough into a rectangle, 3 mm ($\frac{1}{8}$ inch) thick and measuring 30 x 15cm (12 x 6").

8. Spread first with a thin layer of butter and next with some jam, then spread thickly with the filling, leaving a 2.5cm (1-inch) margin all round. Turn in the short ends and roll up into a strudel.

9. Put the strudels, join-side down on a greased or silicone-paper lined tray, leaving room for each strudel to almost double in size when baked. Put the tray in a large plastic bag and leave for 30 minutes or until the strudels are puffy and will spring back when gently pressed with the finger.

10. Preheat the oven to 200°C (400°F/Gas 6). Put the strudels in the oven, turn the heat down to 190°C (375°F/Gas 5) and bake for 25 minutes or until a rich brown.

11. Cool on a wire rack. Just before serving, sprinkle thickly with icing (powdered) sugar.

For the dough:
1 x 6–7g ($\frac{1}{4}$oz) sachet easy-blend (quick-rising) dried yeast
350g (12oz/3 cups) plain (all-purpose) flour
50g (2oz/$\frac{1}{4}$ cup) caster (superfine) sugar
1 tsp salt
200 ml (7 floz/generous $\frac{3}{4}$ cup) hand-hot milk
1 egg yolk
75g (3oz/$\frac{1}{3}$ cup) soft butter

For the filling:
175g (6oz/$1\frac{1}{2}$ cups) ground or whole poppy seeds
175 ml (6 floz/$\frac{3}{4}$ cup) milk
75g (3oz/scant $\frac{1}{2}$ cup) caster (superfine) sugar
finely grated rind of 1 lemon
150g (5oz/1 cup) raisins or sultanas (white raisins)

To spread on the dough:
1 slightly rounded tbsp butter, spreadable or melted
a tart jam such as damson or 'povidl' (continental plum preserve)

For decoration:
sifted icing (powdered) sugar.

Hungarian Mohn Strudel

If you have a light hand making kuchen, do try your hand at making this delicacy.

Parmesan & Poppy Seed Bread

Bread keeps moist (if covered) at room temperature for about 2 days. Freeze for 2 months.

For the dough:
1 x 6–7g (¼oz) sachet easy-
blend (quick-rising) dry
yeast
450g (1 lb/4 cups) strong
white bread flour
1 rounded tbsp granulated
sugar
2 tsp salt
225 ml (8 floz/1 cup) hand
hot water
2 tbsp sunflower (canola)
oil
1 large egg

For the filling:
1 bunch fat spring onions
(green onions), plus 10cm
(4″) of the green stem ,
finely chopped
125g (4oz/½ cup) unsalted
butter
1½ tbsp extra virgin olive oil
3 tbsp grated Parmesan
cheese
4 tbsp poppy seeds

For the glaze:
1 egg yolk, plus 2 tsp water
1 tbsp poppy seeds

This is a winner – a truly wonderful bread which is made with a
challah dough with a filling of poppy seeds, spring onions (green
onions) and cheese cunningly concealed in each strand!

1. Mix the yeast thoroughly with the other dry ingredients,
    then add all the remaining dough ingredients to the bowl of
    an electric mixer.

2. Mix with the dough hook at low speed until a sticky ball
    begins to form, then turn to medium speed and knead for
    4–5 minutes, until the dough is slapping against the edges of
    the bowl, leaving it clean as it goes round. If it looks sticky
    after this time, work in an extra 1 or 2 tablespoons of flour.

3. Tip the dough on to a floured board and knead with the
    hands for a further minute, until it is tight and springy with
    a silky feel – as smooth as a baby's cheek!

4. Grease a large bowl with oil, then turn the dough in it to
    coat it (this stops the surface drying out). Cover with cling-
    film (plastic wrap) and leave to rise in the refrigerator until
    doubled in bulk. If it rises before you have time to deal with
    it (it takes 9–12 hours, but can be left for up to 24 hours),
    punch it down and leave it to rise again. (Chilled dough can
    be quickly 'brought back to life' by giving it two to three 1-
    minute bursts on 'defrost' in a microwave, with 5 minutes
    resting in between each burst.)

5. Meanwhile, prepare the filling. In a medium sauté pan, sauté
    the spring onions in the butter and oil until just limp and
    translucent but not browned, or the filling will be bitter.
    Remove from the heat and stir in the cheese and poppy
    seeds. Cool for 10 minutes.

6. Roll the risen dough into a 45 x 30cm (18 x 12-inch) rectan-
    gle. Cut into 3 strips each 10cm (4″) wide.

7. Spoon one-third of the filling down the centre of each strip, leaving a 2.5cm (1″) border all round. Fold the dough over lengthways and pinch or roll the edges together securely to enclose the filling.

8. On a greased tray, plait the three pieces together fairly loosely and tuck the ends under firmly. Place the tray in a large plastic bag and allow to rise again for 45 minutes or until almost double in bulk. Brush with the glaze and scatter with the seeds.

9. Meanwhile preheat the oven to 190°C (375°F/Gas 5), then bake the bread for 40 minutes, until golden.

10. Cool thoroughly before serving or freezing.

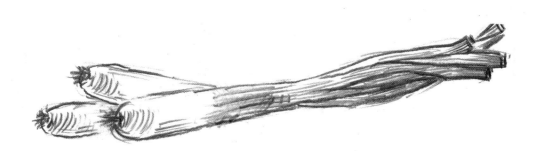

Pesach
Passover

P assover, that great Festival of freedom celebrated for eight days each year, links us directly to our ancestors, those early Israelites who escaped from slavery in Egypt 3,500 years ago and started a 40-year journey across the desert of Sinai, to claim their Promised Land.

Those early Jews fled across the Red Sea together with their families, and it is within our own families today that we celebrate their escape, by eating matzah (unleavened bread), carrying out special food customs, eating once-a-year foods and, perhaps most important, sitting down with families and friends to recall the last meal on Egyptian soil – the Seder.

In addition, Passover is also a Festival of Renewal, a pause after the long winter, to welcome the spring with new ideas and different activities. Because it is essentially a family celebration, it is the one time in the year when everybody in the household has a role to play, whether it is cooking or baking, or preparing the special ceremonial plate and the symbolic foods, to be passed round and eaten by every one, family or guest, seated round the Seder table.

In the not-too-distant past, despite the many helping hands, Pesach was the most labour-intensive Festival in the year, when time-honoured dishes had to be produced from start to finish and mostly by hand – in the family kitchen. Now there is a choice each one of us can make because the grocers' shelves are crammed with 'Kosher for Passover' versions of every possible packeted and fresh food imaginable.

How much of the family's food comes from the food factory and how much is the result of one's own labour is a personal decision – a luxury that wasn't an option until recently. However, don't forget the very special pleasure that can be found in continuing old family customs and making at least some of the traditional dishes. Detailed guides are available from Rabbinical authorities on how to prepare the home and in particular the kitchen for this important Festival.

In this chapter I have gathered together a collection of my tried and trusted recipes for many of the more popular cakes and biscuits, and in particular for those other dishes that are especially suitable to be included in the Seder meal. In addition there are other less familiar ones that could well become part of your family 'minhag'.

Many and varied are the Pesach food customs which have grown up over the centuries and they differ not only between one family and the next, but also between one community of Jews and another. In particular, there are differences between Ashkenazi and Sephardi practices, many of which have arisen because of their geographical location.

For instance, in some Sephardi communities, rice is permitted at Pesach because it is an irreplaceable staple food of the countries where those particular Jews lived for so long. However, it is not permitted in Ashkenazi communities who have potatoes to eat in its stead. Then again, in Sephardi homes it is customary to eat legumes such as peas and beans (known in Hebrew as 'kitniot'). According to the Rabbinical authorities in Britain, 'It is not the custom to eat these foods in the Ashkenazi community' – and a custom practised for many centuries eventually attains the status of a law.

There is a special joy in Pesach cooking, in particular when we prepare the old family recipes such as cinnamon balls and kichels. Many of the cakes and biscuits date from medieval times when there were no artificial raising agents and the lightness of a cake – such as the wonderful sponge cake – depended on how much air could be beaten in by hand.

I hope that the recipes in this chapter will see you through every possible need at Passover. They commence with starters such as the familiar eggs in salt water, and the less familiar Avocado on the Half Shell, or Tuna Pâté with a Cucumber Salad. There's a variety of fish dishes including Salmon Steaks with a Choice of Three Sauces and the visually stunning Salmon Layered with a Herbed Sole Mousse. The selection is on more familiar ground with the exquisite Halibut in Egg and Lemon Sauce. Matzah brei and crispy Chremslach are loved by every family, but why not introduce them to the Sephardi meat and potato casserole, Mina de Pesah?

Chicken is on many people's Seder menu, so you may like to serve Chicken in a fruity Mango Sauce or in a Sweet Pepper and Olive Sauce. Pineapple Chicken makes short tasty work of any leftover bird. There are biscuits galore ranging from Passover Kichels to Choco-walnut Kisses, cakes from the time-honoured Passover Plava, to the innovative Layered Apple Torte. As for the desserts, take your pick from Chocolate Roulade, Peach and Hazelnut Crisp or frozen Coffee Liqueur Parfait with a fresh Pineapple Compôte.

Today we are lucky to have so many electrical 'kitchen maids'.

I have made use of them as much as possible, even in traditional recipes. For instance, lemon curd once took hours to make, being stirred slowly over hot water. Yet by bringing the microwave and the food processor into the preparations, the time taken to produce this delectable preserve can be measured in minutes. An even more onerous job, making apricot 'eingemacht', has all the guess work taken out of it when it can do its bubbling in the microwave.

Setting The Seder Scene

As a young bride, I missed my own family 'minhagim' (customs) when I first sat round the table of my parents-in-law. Their charoset had a different taste, the ceremonial plate was laid out in a different way, and most unexpected of all, there were some strange tunes for the well-loved songs. Soon, however, I began to enjoy the different customs, and then came the year when my husband and I could create our own – though even then I didn't often get my way when it came to the singing!

However many times I prepare the special Sedarim (ceremonial meals), even with the advice written in the Haggadah – the book giving the Order of the Seder Service – I find it enormously helpful to have the details written down for reference, as the menu is planned, the scene is set, and the symbolic foods prepared.

In this chapter, therefore, I shall set the food scene for Pesach, albeit according to the minhag of my own family and the majority of the Anglo-Jewish community.

The Seder Meal

This is very special, because it is conducted according to a particular order of service, which includes partaking of the different symbolic foods that are such an important part of it. This meal is our tribute to those early Jews and the final meal they ate before leaving on their dangerous journey.

Setting the table

Early on the afternoon of Passover Eve, the table is set with a white cloth and the newly burnished candlesticks and their candles are put in place. I find it convenient to leave the table bare during the service that precedes the meal, except for the wine glasses set on little saucers. The cutlery is wrapped in individual napkins so that these can be passed round the guests when the meal is to be served. Elijah's special wine cup sits in the centre of the table.

Now it is time to prepare the ceremonial plate.
The plate itself has given inspiration to many fine craftsmen in ceramic and metal.

In our family, by tradition, preparing the symbolic foods and arranging them on the plate is my husband's privilege – one he has in turn passed on to his sons.

The six symbolic foods
    parsley or lettuce
    salt water
    shankbone of a lamb, usually represented by a grilled
        chicken's neck
    a grilled hard-boiled egg
    a piece of horseradish root
    charoset (see p. 108)

The symbolism of these foods is explained in the Haggadah.

The matzot
The matzot – three pieces of unleavened bread – are concealed in the folds of a table napkin or a special decorated 'matzah dekke', ready for the host to pass pieces around with the ceremonial foods at the appropriate time during the service.

The wine
Four glasses of Kiddush wine are poured during the Seder, but few people drink all four glasses – they are usually just topped up four times instead.

Reclining on cushions
The custom of sitting on cushions and reclining to dine at this special meal is said to have originated in Graeco-Roman times and has continued to this day.

Washing the hands
A bowl, jug of water and a hand towel are placed ready for the ritual washing of the hands during the Seder.

Passover Pastry

Sufficient to fit a 22.5-25cm (9-10 inch) flan dish

150g (5oz/⅔ cup) firm butter
or block margarine
75g (3oz/⅓ cup) potato flour
150g (5oz/⅔ cup) cake meal
or fine matzah meal
50g (2oz/¼ cup) caster
(superfine) sugar
1 beaten egg
1 tbsp lemon juice
1 tsp water

Passover Pastry

This is an excellent Pesach pastry that doesn't need long chilling and is easy to roll out without cracking. It's equally good for jam tarts and coconut or almond slices. As it's so short – and therefore rather fragile – it's better to cook a large tarte in an oven-to-table dish so that it doesn't need lifting out of the tin to serve.

This handles well and can be used for any recipe that calls for shortcrust pastry.

1. Cut the fat into roughly 2.5cm (1-inch) chunks and put in a food processor with the dry ingredients. Pulse 10 times to rub in the fat.

2. Add the egg and liquid and pulse until the mixture is beginning to cling together in little moist balls.

3. Tip out into a bowl, then gather into a ball with the fingers and knead well until smooth and free from cracks.

4. Flatten into a block about 2.5cm (1 inch) thick and chill in the refrigerator for at least 30 minutes. At this stage it can be frozen or refrigerated for 2 days.

Passover Rolls

Makes 12

Eat the same day or freeze for up to 1 month and then defrost as required.

'Crunchy' is the word for these delicious rolls. The recipe is based on choux pastry, substituting matzah meal for the flour in the original.

The raw mixture can be refrigerated overnight, then shaped and baked fresh on the day. Alternatively, it can be shaped into rolls the day before and refrigerated on a baking tray, ready to bake the next day.

1. Mix the meal with the salt and sugar, then set aside.

2. In a 20cm (8-inch) saucepan bring the oil and water to the boil. Then add the meal mixture all at once, stirring vigorously over a low heat until the mixture forms a ball that can be rolled around the pan.

3. Take off the heat and beat in the eggs one at a time (preferably in a food processor or a Kenwood mixer fitted with the 'K' beater) until the mixture is thick and smooth.

4. Leave in a bowl until cool enough to handle – about 30 minutes.

5. Preheat the oven to 190°C (375°F/Gas 5). Grease a baking tray or line with silicone paper.

6. Roll the dough between the palms into 12 balls and place 5cm (2″) apart on the baking trays.

7. Bake for 50 minutes until a rich brown.

225g (8oz/2 cups) fine matzah meal
1 tsp salt
3 tsp sugar
125 ml (4 floz/$\frac{1}{2}$ cup) oil
225 ml (8 floz/1 cup) hot water
4 eggs

EGGS IN SALT WATER

This delicious if unusual dish is only served at this time of year. Whether you give each guest a whole egg and a bowl of the salt water, or slice the egg in the water to make a 'soup', the proportions remain the same.

Allow 1 hard-boiled (hard-cooked) egg per person, with one-third of an egg extra for 'seconds', together with $\frac{1}{2}$ teaspoon of salt dissolved in 150 ml (5 floz/$\frac{2}{3}$ cup) of cold water for each egg used.

Half an hour before the commencement of the Seder, put the salt and water in a very large bowl or tureen, and add the whole shelled eggs, or the sliced eggs. Serve with a soup ladle.

Charoset

Makes 20½ teaspoon servings

Keeps 3 days in the refrigerator.

75g (3oz/¾ cup) walnuts
¼ large cooking apple
sweet kosher (Kiddush)
    wine to moisten
2 level tsp cinnamon
2 level tsp sugar

Charoset

This is my family recipe – a similar mixture is prepared in all Ashkenazi Jewish households whose families originally came from Eastern Europe. However, Sephardim achieve a mortar-like mixture by using other fruits such as dates, apples, oranges, bananas and pears. The Turks, Greeks, Moroccans and Egyptians each have their own recipe, although nuts, cinnamon and wine are common to all.

A large quantity of Charoset – perhaps for a communal Seder – is most quickly made in a food processor. However, my husband, the family Charoset-maker, insists on using a small electric mincer which is used only on this one occasion during the year. Tradition!

The quantity given will be sufficient for 2 Sedarim, each of 8–10 people.

Charoset, is said to have been invented by Rabbi Hillel, who lived between 60 BCE and 9 CE. It is not eaten on any other occasion.

1. Mince the walnuts and the apple.

2. Moisten with the kosher wine and flavour with cinnamon and sugar. The consistency should be that of mortar!

Aubergine & Red Pepper Kugel

Serves 6–8

Keeps 3 days in the refrigerator. Freeze 3 months.

This has a thick, creamy texture with a lovely golden brown crust. With a topping of cheese it can make a main dish for vegetarians; without it, both the dairy and the parev versions can serve as an accompaniment to both meat and fish.

1. Cut off and discard the prickly green calyx, then prick the aubergines all over with a skewer to prevent them bursting.

2. Either bake in the preheated oven for 30 minutes at 230°C (450°F/Gas 8) or place on two thickness of paper towels and microwave on 100 per cent power for 15 minutes . In either case, the aubergines will have begun to collapse and a pointed knife will meet no resistance when plunged into their centres. Leave till cool enough to handle.

3. Preheat the oven to 180°C (350°F/Gas 4). Oil the inside of a gratin dish measuring approximately 25 x 20 x 5cm (10 x 8 x 2inches).

4. Meanwhile, cut the peeled onion and the deseeded pepper into roughly 2.5cm (l-inch) chunks and pulse three times in a food processor until roughly chopped (or chop by hand).

5. Put the olive oil and the vegetables in a lidded pan. Cover and cook over medium heat for 5 minutes, stirring once or twice, until the vegetables have softened and have absorbed the oil.

6. Turn into a mixing bowl and add the basil, pine kernels (if used), salt and pepper.

7. Cut each aubergine in half and scoop out the flesh with a table-spoon. Then either mash or chop by hand, or purée in the food processor.

900 g/2lb aubergines (egg-plants)
1 large onion
1 fat red or orange pepper (bell pepper)
3 tbsp olive oil
2 tbsp thinly sliced fresh basil (about 20 large leaves)
2 rounded tbsp toasted pine kernels (optional)
$1\frac{1}{2}$ tsp salt
20 grinds of black pepper
2 large eggs, lightly beaten
2 rounded tbsp matzah meal
125g (4oz/1 cup) Cheddar cheese, grated (optional)
25g (1oz/2 tbsp) butter or margarine

109

Aubergine & Red Pepper Kugel
continued

8. Add to the onion mixture together with the eggs, whisked until they lighten in colour. Finally, add the matzah meal and mix thoroughly. Taste and add extra salt and pepper if necessary.

9. Turn into the casserole. Cover with the grated cheese (if used) and dot with the butter or margarine.

10. Bake for 35 minutes until golden brown on top.

Avocado on the Half Shell with a Fresh Ginger Dressing

Serves 8–10

For the dressing:
1 tsp each of grated orange and lemon rind
$1\frac{1}{2}$ tbsp lemon juice
4 tbsp orange juice
$\frac{1}{4}$ tsp salt
10 grinds of black pepper
1 tsp caster (superfine) sugar
3 tsp peeled and grated ginger
7 tbsp sunflower (canola) oil
4–5 well ripened avocados

The fruity dressing gives a refreshing start to the Seder.

1. In a screw-top jar, shake all the dressing ingredients together until thickened – 1 minute. Refrigerate.

2. Just before the Seder, cut the avocados in half, remove the stones (pits), then arrange on plates.

3. Shake the dressing well to thicken it again, then divide between the avocados, brushing a little on to the cut surface to stop it browning.

4. Alternatively, slices of peeled avocado can be marinated in the dressing, then arranged on a platter and served with slices of smoked salmon.

Avocado with a Fresh Ginger Dressing

This avocado dish can easily be transformed into a vegetarian main course. Peel, slice and marinate the avocado as described, then arrange it on a bed of mixed greens/salad, accompanied by any of the following: cherry tomatoes, garlic cream cheese, Danish Camembert, stuffed olives, California raisins, roasted salted hazelnuts or almonds, strips of red pepper, sliced button mushrooms and miniature fresh asparagus.

110

Tuna Pâté Hors D'oeuvre with a Cucumber Salad

Serves 6–8

Keeps 5 days in the refrigerator.

Arrange scoops of the tuna on a bed of mixed salad leaves. Garnish with halved cherry tomatoes and the cucumber salad.

1. Put all the pâté ingredients into a food processor and process until smooth. Taste for seasoning. Turn into a small bowl, then cover with clingfilm (plastic wrap) and refrigerate for several hours.

2. To make the salad, thinly slice the unpeeled cucumber with a mandolin or in the food processor.

3. Dissolve the sugar in the boiling water, then add all the remaining dressing ingredients.

4. Pour on to the cucumber slices arranged in a shallow dish.

5. Cover and chill.

large sprig parsley
1 x 200g (7oz) can tuna in oil, drained
175g (6oz/¾ cup) cream cheese
2 fat spring onion (green onion) bulbs, plus 10cm (4″) of the green stem
10 plump black olives, stoned (pitted)
½ tsp paprika
½ tsp salt
10 grinds of black pepper
2 tsp wine vinegar

For the cucumber salad:
1 fat cucumber

For the dressing:
2 level tbsp caster (superfine) sugar
2 tbsp boiling water
4 tbsp wine vinegar
plenty of black pepper
1 tbsp finely cut chives

Whole Salmon Layered with a Herbed Sole Mousse

Serves 6–8 or 10–12 according to size of salmon (photograph between pages 120 and 121)

Fish keeps 4 days in the refrigerator. Freeze leftover fish 1 month.
Sauce keeps 1 week in the refrigerator. Do not freeze.

1 salmon, filleted and
   skinned
fine sea salt

For the mousse:
1 tbsp fresh dill
225g (8oz) skinned and
   filleted lemon sole or plaice
150 ml (5 floz/⅔ cup) chilled
   double (heavy) or whipping cream
1 egg white
1 tsp salt
good pinch of white pepper
grated rind of 2 lemons
2 tsp lemon juice
pinch of sugar
pinch of paprika

For cooking the salmon:
225 ml (8 floz/1 cup) dry
   white wine or fish stock

For the dill and lemon sauce:
425 ml (15 floz/scant 2 cups)
   fish or weak vegetable
   stock
4 egg yolks
1 tbsp potato flour
3 tbsp fresh lemon juice
8 grinds of black pepper
½ tsp salt
3 tsp caster sugar
1 tbsp fresh dill

This is a particularly handsome presentation, with each portion enclosing a slice of the pale green mousse.

Note: a 2–2.5kg (4½–5½lb) fish before filleting, will serve 10–12, a 1.6–1.8kg (3½–4lb) fish will serve 6–8. The filling and the cooking time remain the same.

1. Put the destalked dill into a food processor with the sole or plaice cut into roughly 2.5cm (1-inch) chunks, and process until puréed.

2. Add the cream, egg white, salt, pepper, lemon rind, lemon juice, sugar and paprika, and process only until creamily thickened – about 10 seconds.

3. Preheat the oven to 180°C (350°F/Gas 4).

4. Lightly oil a double thickness of extra wide foil large enough to parcel the salmon, and lay it in a large baking dish.

5. Place one fillet on the foil, lightly salt, then spread with an even layer of the mousse. Lightly salt the second fillet and lay on top of the mousse, re-forming the fish.

6. Heat the wine or stock until steaming (about 1 minute in a microwave), then pour over the fish and seal the foil in a loose parcel to allow the steam to circulate.

7. Bake for 45 minutes, then take out of the oven and leave for 15 minutes.

8. Carefully open the parcel and pour the fish juices into a bowl.

9. Reseal the foil, then leave until cool to the touch. Refrigerate overnight.

10. To make the sauce, make up the fish juices to 425 ml (15 floz) using extra wine or weak vegetable stock.

11. Process all the ingredients except the dill in the food processor for 5 seconds, until thoroughly mixed.

12. Turn into a thick-based pan and stir over a medium heat until the mixture thickens and lightly coats the back of a wooden spoon. Stir in the fresh dill.

13. Leave to thicken overnight in the refrigerator. Serve at room temperature.

Oven-Baked Salmon Steaks with a Choice of Three Sauces

Serves 8

Fish and sauce keep 3 days in the refrigerator.

8 lightly salted salmon
steaks 2cm (¾ inch) thick
125 ml (4 floz/½ cup) white
wine (or 1 tbsp lemon
juice and 75 ml
(3 floz/⅓ cup) water or
vegetable stock)

For garnish:
lemon and lime twists

Any of the three make-ahead sauces marry perfectly with the fish.

1. Preheat the oven to 180°C (350°F/Gas 4). Line a 5cm (2″) deep baking tin large enough to hold the steaks in one layer (or use a foil container with foil), and oil it lightly.

2. Arrange the seasoned steaks side by side in the dish and sprinkle with the liquid. Cover with a 'lid' of foil, sealing it well to the edges of the dish.

3. Bake for 20 minutes. Take out and part the flesh of one of the steaks with a pointed knife to make sure it's an even pale pink right through. If not, give it another 5 minutes.

4. When cool, pour off the liquid and either use it for the lime and watercress sauce or freeze it for a later use. Refrigerate the salmon in the baking dish.

5. Two hours before the Seder, remove the skin and arrange the steaks on a large fish platter or individual plates and leave lightly covered. To serve, garnish with lemon and lime twists and serve with your choice of sauce.

150 ml (5 floz/⅔ cup)
natural yoghurt
225 ml (8 floz/1 cup)
mayonnaise
1 tbsp snipped chives
1 tbsp chopped parsley
pinch of salt and white
pepper

Green Mayonnaise

1. Mix all the ingredients together, then chill until required.

Avocado Salsa

1. Several hours in advance, put the peeled and stoned (pitted) avocados in a food processor or blender, together with all the other ingredients except the yoghurt. Process or blend until smooth, then pulse in the yoghurt.

2. Put in a dish, then cover tightly with clingfilm (plastic wrap) and refrigerate. (If the surface goes a little brown from oxidation, give the salsa a stir just before serving.)

2 x 175g (6oz) or 1 x 275g (10oz) ripe avocados, stoned (pitted)
½ bunch of spring onion (green onion) bulbs
1 medium red pepper (bell pepper)
1 tsp ground coriander
1 tbsp olive oil
2 tbsp lime juice (1–1½ limes, according to size)
½ tsp salt
10 grinds of black pepper
4 tbsp natural yoghurt

For the garnish:
8 sections of lime

Lime and Watercress Sauce

1. If necessary, boil down the cooking liquid from the salmon until it measures 6 tbsp, then allow to cool completely.

2. Put the watercress leaves into a food processor and add the poaching liquid, creams, lime juice and rind, and seasonings, then process until it has thickened to a coating consistency. (By hand, finely chop the watercress leaves then whisk all the ingredients together until of a coating consistency.)

3. Pour into a jug.

75 ml (3 floz/⅓ cup) cooking liquid from the fish
leaves from 2 bunches very fresh watercress
150 ml (5 floz/⅔ cup) double (heavy) cream
150 ml (5 floz/⅔ cup) soured cream or natural yoghurt
juice and grated rind of 1 lime
½ teasp salt
10 grinds of black pepper

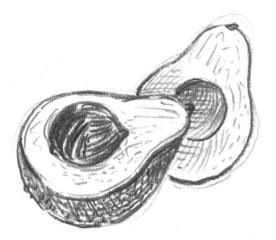

Baked Salmon, 3 Sauces

Poaching in the oven

This method is more convenient than poaching on top of the stove, and it's particularly useful for a Seder meal as the baking tin and contents can simply be transferred to the refrigerator up to 2 days beforehand. Skin, garnish and leave loosely covered at room temperature an hour or so before the Seder.

Salmon under a Pecan or Walnut Crust

Serves 6–8

Serve warm the same day. Alternatively, refrigerate and then serve at room temperature up to 2 days later.

900 g–1.2kg (2–2½ lb) thick
   salmon fillet,
   cut into 6–8 pieces
salt
white pepper
mayonnaise
butter for greasing
   the baking tin

For the crust:
225g (8oz/2 cups) shelled
   pecans or walnut halves
4 tbsp snipped fresh chives
25g (1oz/2 tbsp) butter,
   melted

For the garnish:
lemon quarters

The nut topping keeps the salmon really juicy, whether the fish is served hot or cold.

1. In a food processor, process the nuts until like coarse sand, then mix with the chives and melted butter in a small bowl.

2. Lightly grease with butter a shallow tin wide enough to hold the pieces of salmon in one layer.

3. Arrange them in the tin and season lightly with the salt and pepper, then spread the top of each piece with a thin layer of mayonnaise and cover completely with the nut mixture, patting it on well. Leave until shortly before serving.

4. Fifteen minutes before serving, put in a preheated oven, 220°C (425°F/Gas 7) for 8–10 minutes, or until the salmon flakes easily with a fork. Leave for 10–15 minutes before serving, or refrigerate for use later.

5. Serve garnished with the lemon quarters.

Fillet of Lemon Sole in a Sweet/Sour Tomato & Red Pepper Sauce

Serves 8–10

Serve at room temperature.Leftovers keep 2 days in the refrigerator. Do not freeze.

A richly flavoured sauce complements the fish to perfection.

The dish can be made the day before and refrigerated overnight, but it should be left at room temperature during the first part of the Seder.

1. Sprinkle the washed and skinned fillets lightly with salt, then roll or fold (if very thick) and arrange side by side in a heatproof dish.

2. Preheat the oven to 200°C (400°F/Gas 6).

3. Halve, deseed and cut the pepper into fine slivers. Thinly slice the spring onion bulbs.

4. To make the sauce, heat the oil gently in a heavy saucepan and sauté the spring onion bulbs until softened (about 3 minutes). Then add the tomato and mushroom sauce and remaining sauce ingredients.

5. Bring to the boil, stirring, then pour over the fish. Cover loosely with foil.

6. Bake for 20 minutes, then remove the foil and allow the sauce to bubble for a further 10 minutes.

7. Refrigerate when cold.

8. Two hours before serving, sprinkle with the parsley, cover with the sliced olives and leave at room temperature until required.

1 large or 2 medium fillets of lemon sole per person, skinned

For the sauce:
1 large red pepper (bell pepper)
bunch of spring onion (green onion) bulbs
1 tbsp oil
2 x 300g (11oz) cans Passover tomato and mushroom sauce
1 tbsp tomato purée (paste)
3 tbsp tomato ketchup
2 level tsp each salt and sugar
1 tbsp lemon juice
15 grinds of black pepper

For the garnish:
1 tbsp chopped parsley
125g (4oz/1 cup) sliced stuffed olives

Traditional Halibut in Egg & Lemon Sauce

Serves 6–8

Keeps 4 days in the refrigerator. Do not freeze.

6–8 fillets of baby halibut (675–900 g/1!s–2lb total weight), skinned

For poaching the fish:
water to cover the fish (approx. 425 ml/15 floz/ scant 2 cups)
1 large onion, thinly sliced
3 level tbsp sugar
2 level tsp salt
pinch of white pepper

For the sauce:
225 ml (8 floz/1 cup) of the fish poaching liquor
2 large eggs
4 tbsp fresh lemon juice
2 level tsp potato flour

For the garnish:
sprigs of parsley

After a day in the refrigerator, the fish is permeated with the flavour of the lemon-scented sauce.

1. In a saucepan or lidded frying pan wide enough to hold all the fish in a single layer, bring the water, the onion and the seasonings to the boil. (Adding the sugar at this stage greatly improves the taste of the fish without noticeably sweetening it.)

2. Put in the washed and salted fish steaks. Bring the liquid back to the boil, then lower the heat so that the liquid is barely bubbling. Partially cover the pan and simmer very gently for 20 minutes.

3. Lift out the fish, draining any liquid back into the pan.

4. Place the fish in an oval serving dish about 4cm (1½") deep, then leave to cool while you make the sauce.

5. After the fish has been removed from the pan, boil the fish liquor for 3 minutes to concentrate the flavour. Then strain it and measure out 225 ml (8 floz/1 cup).

6. Mix all the sauce ingredients for 10 seconds in a blender or food processor – this makes it easier to thicken the sauce without fear of it curdling.

7. Put this mixture into a thick-bottomed saucepan and cook gently over low heat until the sauce thickens to the consistency of a coating custard – you will need to stir it constantly. Do not let it boil or the eggs may curdle.

8. Alternatively, cook the sauce in a microwave. Cook the blended ingredients, uncovered, in a microwave-safe jug or bowl on 50 per cent power for 2 minutes. Whisk well, then cook for a further 2–3 minutes, until thickened to the consistency of a coating custard.

9. Taste the sauce and add extra lemon juice if necessary, to make it equally sweet and sour.

10. Pour the sauce over the fish, coating it completely.

11. Leave in the refrigerator overnight, covered with foil.

12. Serve at room temperature, garnished with parsley.

119

Matzah Brei

Serves 3–4

Eat hot off the pan.

2 whole matzot
2 eggs, beaten to blend
pinch of salt
pinch of pepper
25g (1oz/2 tbsp) butter

To serve:
1 tsp ground cinnamon
50g (2oz/¼ cup) caster
   (superfine) sugar

Simply delicious! Pesach breakfast wouldn't be the same without it!

1. Break the matzot into bite-sized pieces and put in a bowl covered with cold water. Soak for 3 minutes, then squeeze out the excess water.

2. Add the matzot to the beaten eggs, with the salt and pepper.

3. Heat the butter in a 17–20cm (7–8-inch) frying pan until it stops foaming, then pour in the mixture and pat into a large pancake shape. Cook over moderate heat until golden brown, then turn and brown the second side.

4. Cut into 3–4 wedge-shaped pieces and serve plain or with the mixture of cinnamon and sugar.

These crisp little fritters probably date back to Biblical times.

Opposite: potato latkes (page 70)
Over left: Sutganiyot (Israeli-style doughnuts) (page 80)
rugelach (page 78)
and fruitcake (page 77)
Over right: Hammentaschen with a prune and walnut filling (page 92)
and ras tahini (page 97)
Centre left: Whole salmon with sole mousse (page 112)
Centre right: Chicken in a mango sauce (page 127)

Chremslach (Matzah Meal Pancakes)

Serves 3–4

Eat hot off the pan.

They're delicious to eat sprinkled with cinnamon sugar (1 tsp cinnamon mixed with 50g (2oz/¼ cup) caster sugar) for a lazy Sunday breakfast.

1. Whisk the eggs, salt and 2 tablespoons of the water until thick.

2. Gradually stir in the matzah meal and the sugar, followed by the remaining water.

3. Allow the batter to stand and thicken for 10 minutes.

4. Fry tablespoonfuls of the mixture in hot oil about 5 mm (¼ inch) deep until crisp and puffed on top then turn and cook the other side.

3 large eggs
1 level tsp salt
approx. 150 ml (5 floz/⅔ cup) water
75g (3oz/¾ cup) fine matzah meal
1½ level tbsp caster (superfine) sugar
oil for frying

Previous left: cinnamon balls (page 139)
*   and coconut pyramids (page 140)*
*   and choco-walnut kisses (page 141)*
Previous right: savoury cheese cake with olives and anchovies (page 169)
Opposite: cheese cake with kumquats (page 180)
*   and cream cheese blintzes with sour cherries (page 174)*

Cheese, Tuna & Matzah 'Lasagne'

Serves 4–6

May be reheated.

4 whole matzot
1 x 225g (8oz) pack frozen
  leaf spinach, thawed
1 medium onion, peeled
  and finely chopped
1 fat clove of garlic, peeled
  and finely chopped
25g (1oz/2 tbsp)
  butter or margarine
1 x 425g (15oz) can
  chopped tomatoes or
  2 x 225g (8oz)
  cans tomato sauce
1 tsp salt
good pinch of black pepper
1 can tuna, well drained
  and flaked
oil for brushing the inside
  of the dish
2 eggs, beaten
175g (6oz/1½ cups) Cheddar
  cheese, grated

Cheese, Tuna 'Lasagne'

This is a modern version of the Sephardi Mina de Pesah, which is made in innumerable variations, both meat and milk, by Jews from the former Ottoman Empire. However, common to all the recipes are layers of soaked matzot, which are used to simulate lasagne pasta.

Omit the tuna from this version, and you have an excellent vegetarian main dish.

1. Preheat the oven to 190°C (375° F/Gas 5).

2. Soak the matzot in warm water to cover for 3 minutes, then lift out carefully and lay on paper towels to drain.

3. Drain the spinach by putting it in a sieve and pressing hard on it. Chop coarsely.

4. In a large frying pan, cook the onion and the garlic in the butter over medium heat until soft and golden. Add the tomatoes and juice (or the tomato sauce), together with the spinach, salt and pepper. Cook stirring occasionally, until thick but still juicy, then stir in the flaked tuna and set aside until it stops steaming.

5. Brush the oil over the bottom and sides of a 20–22.5cm (8–9 inch) square baking tin, foil container or ovenproof glass dish about 5cm (2″) deep.

6. Beat the eggs to blend, then put on a large platter. Lift one matzah and carefully coat it with the egg, then lay in the bottom of the baking dish, using part of a second coated matzah to cover the bottom completely. Spread half of the tuna/vegetable mixture on top and sprinkle with one third of the grated cheese. Repeat with more coated matzot the remainder of the tuna mixture and another third of the cheese. Finally cover with the remaining coated matzot and sprinkle with the rest of the cheese.

7. Bake for 20–25 minutes until the cheese is melted and golden and the casserole is bubbling nicely. Take out and leave to rest for 5–10 minutes before serving in squares.

To reheat:
10. Cover loosely with foil and reheat at the same temperature for 15 minutes or until bubbly. If it is cooked in a glass dish, it can be reheated, uncovered, in the microwave on full power until bubbly – about 3 minutes.

Pastel de Kwezo (Salonika Herbed Cheese Pie)

Serves 6–8

Leftovers keep 2 days in the refrigerator, but need recrisping under a moderate grill (broiler).

The contrast between the creamily set filling and the crispy topping is mouth-watering.

1. Preheat the oven to 190°C (375°F/Gas 5).

2. Select a baking dish the width of one matzah and the length of two (approx. 30 x 17 x 5cm/12 x 7 x 2"). With a different sized dish (or foil container) you will need to patch the matzot.

3. Soak the matzot in milk for 3–5 minutes, or until pliable but not soggy. Drain off the milk and blot each matzah in turn with paper towels to remove excess moisture.

4. Brush the bottom and sides of the dish with melted butter.

5. Whisk the eggs until fluffy. Put the cheese into a large bowl and gradually stir in the eggs, followed by the herbs and seasonings. It should be highly seasoned.

6. Line the bottom of the dish with two softened matzot side by side, then brush generously with some of the melted butter. Lay another layer of matzot on top and carefully spoon the cheese mixture over these in an even layer. Arrange another two matzot on top, brush with butter as before, then cover with the remaining matzot and butter them.

7. Bake for 35–40 minutes or until the filling is set and the top is a golden brown. Leave at least 10 minutes before cutting into squares.

8. If preferred, serve at room temperature on the same day.

8 matzot
milk
75g (3oz/¾ cup) melted butter
4 eggs, beaten
675g (1½ lb/3 cups) curd (medium- to low-fat) cheese
2 tbsp finely snipped chives
25g (1oz/½ cup) each chopped fresh dill and mint
1½ tsp salt
25 grinds of black pepper

Pastel De Kwezo

This delicious Sephardi 'bake' is inspired by a recipe in the *Cookbook of the Jews of Greece* (Nicholas Stravonlakis, Lycabettus Press) The original version mixed a couple of tablespoons of sesame seeds with the cheese, but as these are considered 'kitniot' and not for use in Ashkenazi homes during Pesach, I have omitted them. The filling needs lots of fresh herbs and seasoning to achieve the right degree of 'ta'am' (good flavour).

Mina de Carne

Serves 4–6 as a main course, 8 as a side dish

Prepare and bake the same day. Leftovers keep 3 days in the refrigerator.

4 whole matzot
2 tbsp pine kernels
  (optional)
1 tbsp oil
1 fat clove of garlic, peeled
  and finely chopped
1 medium onion, peeled
  and finely chopped
2 celery sticks, finely sliced
425g (15oz/4 cups) lean
  minced (ground) beef
2 tbsp chopped parsley
1 tbsp tomato ketchup
1 tsp salt
30 grinds of black pepper
425g (15oz) potatoes,
  boiled and mashed
3 eggs
3 tbsp oil

A delicious Passover version of lasagne.

1. Soak the unbroken matzot in cold water for 2 minutes until soft, then lift out on to paper towels and blot thoroughly to remove as much moisture as possible.

2. Lightly fry the pine kernels (if used) in the oil, then drain on a paper towel.

3. In the same fat, sauté the garlic, onion and celery until golden. Add the meat and cook, stirring with a fork to break it up, until it is a rich brown. Add the pine kernels, parsley, ketchup, salt and pepper.

4. Turn the meat mixture into a bowl and stir in the mashed potatoes and two of the eggs, well beaten.

5. Preheat the oven to 200°C (400°F/Gas 6). Brush an oven-to-table dish about 4cm (1¾") deep (a gratin-type or a foil container is excellent) with 1½ tablespoons of the remaining oil.

6. Cover the base with two of the matzot (if necessary, patch to fit). Cover with the meat mixture, then lay the other two matzot on top and brush with the rest of the oil beaten with the remaining egg.

7. Bake for 45–50 minutes or until set and golden brown.

8. Serve cut into squares.

Succulent Roast Chicken with an Apricot Stuffing

Serves 6

Leftovers keep 3 days under refrigeration. Freeze 3 months.

To keep the breast meat juicy, the bird is cooked breast-side down and turned over to complete the browning only for the last 30 minutes. When calculating the cooking time, allow an extra 15 minutes for the bird to 'settle' out of the oven before it is carved.

1. Preheat the oven to 200°C (400°F/Gas 6).

2. Cover the cut-up apricots generously with water and cook on 100 per cent power in a microwave for five minutes. Without a microwave, cover with water as before, but use a small lidded pan. Simmer, covered, for 10 minutes, then leave to cool.

3. Crumble the matzot as finely as possible into a large basin. Add 175 ml (6 floz/¾ cup) of the soaking liquid from the apricots (add water or stock if necessary to make up the quantity), then leave to soften.

4. Meanwhile, cook the onion in the margarine until softened and golden.

5. Add the seasonings, lemon rind and juice, chopped parsley and the beaten egg to the matzah, then add to the onions in the pan and cook gently until the matzah starts to brown and loses some of its wetness.

6. Stir in the well-drained apricots and mix well.

7. Stuff the cavity of the bird.

8. In a roasting tin that will just hold the bird comfortably, put a poultry cradle or grilling (broiling) rack.

9. Make a shallow nick on each side of the bird where the leg joint meets the breast, and insert half the peeled clove of garlic in each.

1 x 2–2.25kg (4½–5lb)
  chicken
1 fat clove of garlic, peeled
olive oil for brushing the
  bird
sea salt and black pepper
300 ml (10 floz/1¼ cups)
  strong chicken stock,
  home-made or use 1 stock
  (bouillon) cube and water

For the stuffing:
125g (4oz/¾ cup) tenderized
  dried apricots, each half
  cut into 4
125g (4oz) matzot
175 ml (6 floz/¾ cup) soaking water from apricots
1 large onion, finely
  chopped
50g (2oz/¼ cup) margarine
½ tsp salt
¼ tsp white pepper
½ tsp paprika
grated rind of half a large
  lemon
good squeeze of lemon
  juice
1 tbsp chopped parsley
1 large egg

For the gravy:
2 tsp potato flour
2 tbsp water or white wine

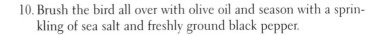

Succulent Roast Chicken with an Apricot Stuffing
continued

> ### Succulent Chicken With An Apricot Stuffing
>
> This could be the time when you invest in a poultry cradle, which keeps the chicken from absorbing the fat as it melts from the skin while roasting.

10. Brush the bird all over with olive oil and season with a sprinkling of sea salt and freshly ground black pepper.

11. Pour the hot stock into the roasting tin, then lay the bird upside down on it (if it doesn't sit comfortably, arrange it on its side).

12 Roast it this way for 20 minutes per 450g (1 lb), plus 30 minutes – for a 2.25kg (5lb) stuffed bird, the total cooking time will be 2 hours 10 minutes.

13. Baste the bird every 30 minutes with the stock, then 30 minutes before the end of the cooking time, turn it over (a large wooden or metal spoon inserted in the cavity makes the job easier) and cook breast-side up for the remaining time.

14. Lift it on to a carving dish or board, then cover lightly with foil (to retain the heat).

15. Pour off any free fat and if the stock has dried up, add enough boiling water to bring it back to the original 300 ml (10 floz/1¼ cups). Stir well to loosen any of the crispy bits on the bottom of the tin, then pour into a small pan and add the potato flour mixed to a cream with the water or white wine.

16. Bring to the boil and simmer for 3 minutes, but do be sure to taste it and correct the seasoning if necessary. If the fat content of the meal has a high priority, discard the (alas, delectable) skin – this will halve the calorie content of each serving!

Chicken in a Mango Sauce:

Serves 8

Keeps 3 days in the refrigerator. Freeze 3 months.

Juicy joints of chicken are cooked in a refreshing fruit sauce flavoured with fresh ginger.

1. Preheat the oven to 160°C (325°F/Gas 3).

2. Put the matzah meal, ground ginger, and the 1 teaspoon salt in a medium plastic bag and shake each chicken portion in it one at a time to coat it.

3. Fry the joints in the hot oil until golden brown on all sides. Remove to a roasting tin or casserole large enough to hold the portions side by side.

4. To the oil in the pan, add the nut of margarine and cook the finely chopped shallots and garlic gently until soft and golden. Stir in the cumin (if used), chopped ginger, wine, stock, the peeled and coarsely chopped mango, the salt and pepper. Stir well, then bring to the boil.

5. Pour over and round the chicken. Cover and cook for 40–50 minutes or until cooked through. There will be no sign of pink when a portion is nicked to the bone with a small pointed knife.

6. Lift out the chicken on to a serving dish and keep warm, covered with foil in the oven turned down to 140°C (275°F/Gas 1) for up to 30 minutes.

7. Purée the contents of the oven dish in a blender or food processor and thin with a little extra stock if necessary, until of a coating consistency.

8. Before serving, reheat this sauce, pour some over the chicken and save the rest to serve at the table.

9. Garnish the chicken with slices of the remaining mango and serve with the rest of the sauce.

2 tbsp fine matzah meal
½ tsp ground ginger
1 tsp salt
8 chicken portions
4 tbsp oil
nut of margarine
4 shallots
2 cloves of garlic
1 tsp cumin (optional)
2.5cm (1-inch) piece of fresh ginger, peeled and chopped
300 ml (10 floz/1¼ cups) white wine
300 ml (10 floz/1¼ cups) chicken stock
2 large ripe mangoes (save half of one for garnish)
½ tsp salt
10 grinds black pepper

Chicken in a Mango Sauce

To reheat a chicken casserole during the Seder, cover and leave in a slow oven, 150°C (300°F/Gas 2). Check at the start of the meal and if it is not steaming hot and on the point of bubbling, turn the oven up to 160°C (325°F/Gas 3) during the earlier part of the meal.

Baked Breasts of Chicken in a Crunchy Coating

Serves 8

Keeps 3 days in the refrigerator.
The boned breasts (or bone-in joints) can be frozen ready for the oven for up to a month.
Thaw in the refrigerator overnight, then cook as though freshly prepared.

4 tbsp fresh lemon juice
  (approx. 2 large lemons)
8 x 125–150g (4–5oz) part-
  boned chicken breasts
  with wing
oil for baking tray

For the coating:
3 heaped tbsp each matzah
  meal and fine meal
1 egg
4 tbsp oil
1 tbsp each finely chopped
  fresh tarragon and parsley
1 tsp salt
20 grinds of black pepper

Baked Breasts Of Chicken In A Crunchy Coating

Most marinades contain some kind of acid such as wine, vinegar of lemon juice, as well as herbs and spices. In addition – and this is particularly important with meat – the acid helps to break down and tenderize the tougher cuts.

On the other hand, macerating is a method used to imbue fruit with the flavour of a sweet liquid, often containing spirits such as rum or brandy or a fruity liqueur.

These processes are an easy way of maximising both savoury and sweet flavours – provided you remember to do it in good time!

Cooked this way, boned chicken breasts stay really succulent. Ask the butcher to skin them and remove the ribs, but leave the wing on. The breasts then have a better shape. Alternatively, joints on the bone can be used instead (see cooking instructions below).

1. Up to 4 hours in advance (but not less than 1 hour) grate the yellow zest from 1 lemon and reserve for the coating. Put the lemon juice in a shallow dish and lay the breasts in it, turning them once or twice whilst marinating.

2. Preheat the oven to 220°C (425°F/Gas 7).

3. Spread the mixed matzah and fine meals on a baking tray and leave in the oven as it heats up, until a golden brown – about 15 minutes – stirring once or twice. Take out and leave to cool.

4. In a shallow bowl, whisk together the egg and oil and stir in the chopped herbs.

5. In another dish mix together the meal, lemon rind, salt and pepper.

6. Lightly oil a baking tray.

7. Brush the chicken breasts evenly with the egg and oil mixture, then roll in the meal.

8. Bake for 25 minutes or until they are golden brown, crisp and just cooked through. (Nick one to check there's no sign of pink – if necessary allow another 5 minutes.)

9. If using bone-in chicken joints, cook for 35–40 minutes (depending on size) at 200°C (400°F/Gas 6).

Chicken in a Sweet Pepper & Olive Sauce

Serves 8–10

Will keep 3 days in the refrigerator. Freeze 3 months.

Reheating the dish for the Seder actually improves the flavour.

1. Preheat the oven to 180°C (350°F/Gas 4).

2. Coat the chicken portions in the seasoned matzah meal. Heat the oil in a sauté pan and fry the chicken pieces until golden brown, then drain on paper towels. Transfer to a casserole large enough to hold the joints in one layer.

3. In the same oil sauté the peppers with the garlic and onion until golden. Add all the remaining ingredients and simmer uncovered until the sauce is thickened but still juicy.

4. Pour over the chicken joints – it should half cover them. Add an extra splash of wine if necessary. Cover with a lid or foil and cook for 45 minutes, basting once.

5. Taste and add salt and pepper if necessary. Allow to cool, then refrigerate.

6. Leave for 1 hour at room temperature, then reheat during the Seder at 160°C (325°F/Gas 3) until bubbling.

7. Just before serving scatter with the olives and sprinkle with the parsley.

8–10 chicken portions, skinned
1 heaped tbsp fine matzah meal
1 tsp salt
20 grinds of black pepper
3 tbsp oil
2 each large red and yellow peppers (bell peppers), deseeded and sliced in strips
4 cloves of garlic, chopped
2 large onions, thinly sliced
2 x 400g (14oz) or 1 x 800g (29oz) can peeled tomatoes, roughly chopped if whole
1 tbsp sugar
425 ml (15 floz/scant 2 cups) chicken stock
200 ml (7 floz/generous $\frac{3}{4}$ cup) ($\frac{1}{4}$ bottle) red wine
1 rounded tbsp tomato purée (paste)
2 tsp paprika

For garnish:
125g (4oz/1 cup) pitted black olives
1 tbsp chopped parsley

Chicken in a Sweet Pepper and Olive Sauce

The variety of olives available is enormous: green or black, small and sweet, large and fleshy, with or without stones (pits), or stuffed. I prefer black olives because, unlike the green ones which are picked unripe, they are ripened on the tree so that the flavour can develop its full potential.

Pineapple Chicken

Serves 6

Leftovers keep 2 days in the refrigerator. Freeze 1 month.

2 tbsp oil
2 tbsp coarsely chopped
   blanched almonds
1 medium onion, peeled,
   halved, then very thinly
   sliced
1 large red pepper (bell
   pepper), deseeded and
   very thinly sliced
350g (12oz/1½ cups) cooked
   chicken (about half a
   cooked medium-sized
   bird), cut into bite-sized
   chunks
1 x 225g (8oz) can pineapple, cut up into small
   chunks
1 tsp potato flour
1 level tbsp demerara
   (brown) sugar
2 tsp vinegar
150 ml (5 floz/⅔ cup) syrup
   from pineapple
1 chicken stock (bouillon)
   cube

A delicious dish for Chol Hamoed – to serve accompanied by boiled new potatoes, or oven-baked ones.

1. Heat the oil and cook the almonds until golden. Lift out with a slotted spoon and drain on paper towels.

2. In the same oil, cook the onion until softened but not browned (about 5 minutes), then add the red pepper and cook for a further 3 minutes.

3. Add the chicken and the pineapple, and allow to heat through gently.

4. Put the potato flour in a small bowl, then add the sugar, vinegar and pineapple syrup. Crumble the chicken stock cube and add.

5. Add to the chicken mixture in the pan and simmer for 3 minutes. Taste for seasoning. Stir in the almonds. May be reheated until bubbling.

Lemon Lamb

There's surely no other ethnic food culture which demands that those who cook for their families must once a year pay heed to rulings laid down nearly 2,000 years ago! Yet it was in the first century of this era, after the destruction of the Second Temple, that roast lamb was banished from the place it had held in the Seder menu ever since the Children of Israel were ordered to eat roast lamb with their matzah and bitter herbs (Exodus 12.8). Once there was no Temple – and therefore no sacrifices of a year-old lamb – the Rabbis changed the menu, and lamb was out. Some communities do not eat lamb at all during Pesach week; others actually make a point of serving it (other than at the Seder), and this is now the general custom amongst Ashkenazi communities in Britain.

The deeper flavours of a more mature animal can be given a spring-like flavour with the juice of a lemon and – most important – the yellow zest which contains the essential citrus flavouring oil. I have discovered that unwaxed lemons – albeit more expensive – seem to be a variety with a wonderfully perfumed zest.

Lemon Lamb

Serves 6–8

Keeps 3 days in the refrigerator. Freeze 1 month (after which the spicing may fade).

A superb dish for Chol Hamoed. You will find the flavour deepens considerably if you cook the casserole one day and reheat it not less than 24 hours later.

1. At least 2 hours before cooking, whisk together in a bowl all the marinade ingredients. Add the meat and turn well to coat it, then leave to marinate, turning two or three times.

2. Preheat the oven to 150°C (300°F/Gas 2).

3. Remove the lamb with a slotted spoon, reserving any remaining marinade.

4. Brush with oil a heavy sauté pan or casserole and when very hot, brown the lamb on all sides. Add the onions and scatter with the potato flour. Brown for a further minute or two, then add the marinade and pour on enough chicken stock barely to cover. Bring to simmering point over a moderate heat.

5. Transfer to the oven. Cover and cook for about 1½ hours or until the lamb is meltingly tender, adding the mushrooms for the last 30 minutes. Remove from the oven.

6. If the juice is too thin (the mushrooms will have given out some liquid), remove the meat with a slotted spoon, then reduce the sauce by boiling fast until it is nicely thickened and has a rich flavour. Add some lemon juice – you will probably need 2–3 teaspoons – and extra salt and pepper if necessary, then pour over the meat.

7. Cool, then refrigerate overnight.

8. To serve, reheat until piping hot throughout, either on top of the stove, in a moderate oven or in a microwave.

9. Serve scattered with the almonds and chopped herb, accompanied by boiled new potatoes.

1.5–1.8kg (3–4 lb) boned shoulder of lamb cut into approx. 2.5cm (1-inch) cubes

For the marinade:
3 tbsp olive or vegetable oil
4 cloves of garlic, finely chopped
2 lemons
1 tsp salt
20 grinds of black pepper
1 tsp ground cumin
2 tsp ground coriander
½ tsp ground ginger
1 rounded tbsp slivered fresh ginger

For cooking the lamb:
2 onions, finely chopped
1 tbsp potato flour
425 ml (15 floz/scant 2 cups) hot chicken stock
225g (8oz/2½ cups) button mushrooms
sea salt and freshly ground black pepper to taste

For the garnish:
25g (1oz/¼ cup) toasted flaked (slivered) or chopped almonds
chopped parsley or coriander (cilantro)

La Tegamata (Beef and Potato Casserole)

Serves 6–7

Keeps 3 days in the refrigerator. Freeze 3 months.

1.3kg (2¾ lb) (trimmed weight) best braising steak, cut into 2cm (1-inch) cubes

For the marinade:
225 ml (8 floz/1 cup) dry red wine
1 medium carrot and 1 medium onion, both peeled and cut into small dice or roughly chopped on a food processor
a sprig of fresh rosemary or ½ tsp dried rosemary
strips of zest from half an orange
3 whole cloves or pinch of ground cloves

For cooking the meat:
3 tbsp olive oil
1 fat clove of garlic, sliced thinly
2 tsp salt
3 tsp demerara sugar
pinch of mild chilli pepper or cayenne pepper
1 x 400g (14oz) can chopped tomatoes
about 20 cooked new potatoes

I prefer to cook La Tegamata in the oven as it needs far less attention than when simmered on top of the stove as in the original Italian-Jewish recipe.

1. Several hours in advance or the night before, put the cubes of meat in a fairly shallow container, then mix the marinade ingredients and pour over them. Mix well, then leave in the refrigerator for 5 hours or overnight, stirring occasionally.

2. Strain the meat from the liquid and dab as dry as possible with paper towels. Reserve the liquid.

3. Preheat the oven to 150°C (300°F/Gas 2).

4. Heat the olive oil in a heavy frying or sauté pan and brown the meat on all sides, together with any vegetables clinging to it – it's actually quicker to do this in two batches as too much meat in the pan will produce a lot of moisture and hinder the browning process.

5. Remove the meat to an ovenproof casserole.

6. Pour the marinade into the sauté pan together with the garlic, salt, sugar and chili pepper or cayenne. Bubble for 4 minutes to concentrate the flavour, then add the canned tomatoes. Bring to the boil again, then pour over the beef. It should just cover the meat. If not, add a little extra wine.

7. Cover and transfer to the oven and cook for 30 minutes, or until bubbles are breaking the surface. Turn the oven down to 140°C (275°F/Gas 1) for a further 2 hours, or until the meat is meltingly tender.

8. Add the cooked potatoes to the casserole 10 minutes before the meat is cooked.

132

Stracotto (A Joint of Beef Cooked in Wine)

Serves 6–7

Keeps 3 days in the refrigerator. Freeze 3 months.

This uses the same marinade ingredients and a similar method to the Tegamata, but with a 1.8kg (4 lb) corner of chuck (bola in the North of England) instead of the cubed braising steak.

1. Marinate the meat for a full 24 hours, as it takes longer for the flavours to be absorbed by a joint.

2. Preheat the oven to 150°C (300°F/Gas 2)

3. Cook the joint with the marinade in a casserole for 3 hours. If the liquid starts to bubble fiercely, turn the heat down to 140°C (275°F/Gas 1).

4. When the joint is cooked (it will 'give' when pressed), lift it on to a heatproof plate, cover lightly with foil and return to the oven turned down to its lowest temperature.

5. Now it's time to deal with the sauce. The juices in the casserole can be puréed either in a food processor or blender, then reheated until bubbling.

With An Italian Accent
La Tegamata

According to Dr Luciano Tas, editor of the Italian Jewish magazine Shalom, there are records of the existence of a Jewish community in Rome as far back as 159 BCE with a great influx from Spain and Portugal in the late fifteenth century. As with every other 'ethnic' Jewish cuisine, the Italian Jews have developed a way of cooking that combines dishes from the host country, suitably modified, with others they brought from their original birthplace.

Dipping into *The Classic Cuisine of the Italian Jews* (Edda Servi Machlin, Giro Press, New York), I came across such delicacies as 'Ceciarchiata' which Ashkenazim know as 'Teiglach'; 'Matzah Coperta', an exotic version of that old favourite 'Matzah Brei', but including pine kernels and raisins, and the famous Italian Jewish dish, 'Carciofi alla Giudea' (artichokes, Jewish style).

Far more familiar is a dish of marinated beef. This is very similar to the daubes and stews of other Mediterranean cuisines, save for its flavouring of cloves, rosemary and chilli pepper. I've made some amendments to the original recipe called La Tegamata – to suit our British palates and cooking methods – and have tried it both as a casserole, using best braising steak, and as a joint, using corner of chuck (bola), when it's known as Stracotto. In both dishes, the meat is marinated in wine, which gives it a glorious flavour.

Apricot Eingemacht (Microwave Method)

Makes 675–900g (1?1/2–2 lb)

Keeps 6 months in the refrigerator.

250g (9oz/1 ¾ cups) tenderized dried apricots, split
  in half if whole
water barely to cover
3 tbsp lemon juice
450g (1 lb/2 cups) granulated sugar
50g (2oz/½ cup) split
  blanched almonds
  (optional)

An easy way to make this traditional conserve if you don't enjoy the conventional jam-making method on top of the stove.

To produce a diabetic version of the Apricot Eingemacht, use exactly the same method, but substitute 225g (8oz/1 cup) fructose for the 450g (1 lb/2 cups) of granulated sugar used in the regular recipe.

1. Put the apricots into a microwave-safe lidded casserole, then pour on cold water to cover. Cover and cook on 100 per cent power in the microwave for 5 minutes.

2. Lift the apricots out of the liquid with a draining spoon and put in a 2.25-litre (4-pint/2-quart) Pyrex bowl.

3. Add the cooking liquid (approximately 175 ml/6 floz/¾ cup), the lemon juice, sugar and almonds (if used).

4. Cook uncovered in the microwave on 100 per cent power for 3 minutes, then stir well to ensure the sugar is dissolved.

5. Cook uncovered for a further 15 minutes, until the apricots are bubbling in a syrup which coats the back of a wooden spoon (the mixture should have been bubbling fiercely for 10 minutes). Take out of the microwave.

6. Put 4 tablespoons of cold water in each of two clean 450g (1 lb) jam jars and bring to the boil, uncovered, on 100 per cent power – about 1½ minutes. Then turn upside down to drain and dry on paper towels. After 30 seconds turn right-side up. Alternatively, leave the empty jars in a low oven for 10 minutes until very hot.

7. Fill with the conserve and screw on the lids.

Beetroot Eingemacht

Makes nearly 3.25kg (7 lb) – enough to share with family and friends

Keeps 6 months in the refrigerator.

This traditional beetroot conserve must be cooked until it goes brown – a sign that the sugar in the beetroot has caramelized, giving the jam its inimitable flavour. If you have patience, this is a foolproof method, even for the inexperienced jam-maker.

1. Boil the uncooked beetroot in water to cover for 1 hour, then cool and skin.

2. Cut the cooked beetroot into slivers 1cm ($\frac{3}{8}$ inch) wide and 2.5–5cm (1–2″) long (or use the julienne cutter on a food processor).

3. Put into a large bowl with the sugar. Mix well, then leave overnight.

4. Next day, put the sugar/beetroot mixture into a very large, heavy pan, together with the lemon segments.

5. Bring to the boil, stirring, until the sugar has dissolved. Then leave to bubble over a low heat, stirring occasionally, for at least 3 hours, until the mixture loses its redness and the beetroot becomes translucent and starts to turn brown.

6. Finally, add the almonds and the smaller amount of ginger. Taste – but be careful, it's hot – and add the extra ginger if you wish.

7. Bubble for a further 15 minutes.

8. Prepare 7 x 450g (1lb) jam jars as in the Apricot Eingemacht recipe and fill with the hot conserve.

2.25kg (5 lb) uncooked beetroot (beets)
1.8kg (4 lb/9 cups) granulated sugar
3 large lemons, peeled and segmented like an orange
175g (6oz/1½ cups) split almonds
25–40g (1–1½oz/3–4 tbsp) ground ginger

Lemon & Passion Fruit Curd (Microwave method)

Makes approx. 575g (1¼ lb)

Keeps 3 months in the refrigerator.

finely grated rind of 3
    lemons
175 ml (6 floz/¾ cup) lemon
    juice (about 3 large
    lemons)
3 passion fruit
75g (3oz/⅓ cup) butter
225g (8oz/1 cup) caster
    (superfine) sugar
3 whole eggs

The passion fruit may not be traditional, but it does add a wonderful new flavour dimension to the curd!

1. Two hours in advance, put the rind to soak in the lemon juice to extract the flavouring oils. After 2 hours pour this mixture through a sieve, then discard the rind.

2. Halve the passion fruit, turn the pulp into a sieve placed over the bowl of lemon juice, then press hard to extract as much juice as possible. Discard the black seeds.

3. In a large microwave-safe jug or bowl, melt the butter at 100 per cent power for 1 minute (cover lightly with a paper towel to prevent spattering).

4. Stir in the lemon juice and sugar and cook uncovered on 100 per cent power for 2 minutes. Then stir again to ensure that the sugar is dissolved in the liquid.

5. In a food processor or blender, process the eggs to blend for 10 seconds, then slowly add the hot, buttery liquid through the feed tube, processing all the time.

6. Return the mixture to the jug and microwave on 100 per cent power for 2½ minutes, stirring halfway.

7. Take out and stir vigorously to ensure the curd is even in texture – it should be the consistency of a thick coating custard. If not, cook for a further 30 seconds.

8. Have ready two washed and rinsed 225g (8oz) jars, plus a small soufflé or jam dish, heated as for the Apricot Eingemacht.

9. Fill the hot jars to the brim with the curd, then cover and refrigerate when cold. The remainder can be put in the smaller dish as a 'taster'.

Citrus-Scented Macaroons

Makes 15–20

Keep 1 week in the refrigerator in an airtight container. Freeze 1 month.

These have a delightful fruitiness.

1. Preheat the oven to 200°C (400°F/Gas 6) and line two baking trays with silicone paper.

2. By hand or machine, mix the ground almonds and icing sugar, together with the grated fruit rinds. Add most of the egg whites, reserving two tablespoonsful for coating, and beat or process until a Plasticine-like soft dough is formed. Add some of the remaining egg white only if necessary to achieve the right consistency.

3. Pinch off pieces the size of a small walnut, then roll in the hands, forming small balls. In a basin mix the reserved egg white with a teaspoon of cold water and whisk with a fork until frothy. Mix the almonds and sugar together in another bowl. Dip the balls in the egg white, then in the almond and sugar mixture. Arrange on the trays about 5cm (2″) apart.

4. Bake for 12 minutes, until light gold on top and firm to the touch – inside they will have the typical moist texture of macaroons. Remove from the trays and allow to cool.

125g (4oz/1 cup) ground almonds
125g (4oz/½ cup) icing (powdered) sugar
grated rind of half a large lemon
grated rind of half a large orange
2 egg whites (reserve 2 tbsp for coating)

For coating the biscuits:
2 tbsp blanched almonds, chopped
2 tbsp caster (superfine) sugar
reserved egg white

Lemon Curd

I have a little pottery jar shaped like a beehive which has symbolized Pesach in my family for at least three generations. Every year I fill it with home-made lemon curd – as my mother and grandmother did before me, using a recipe that dates from the early years of the twentieth century.

A recipe for lemon curd similar to the one my mother used appears in *The Jewish Cookery Book* of 1895, written by a Miss Tattersall for use in the Cookery Centres under the School Board of London. Jewish cook books such as this one, written in the late nineteenth and early twentieth century, contain few recipes we would consider 'haimishe', but were part of a concerted attempt to Anglicize the children of Jewish immigrants by teaching them English dishes such as lemon curd. The plan certainly worked because making lemon curd soon became, together with the traditional eingemacht of Eastern Europe, an essential part of Pesach preparation in every Anglo-Jewish kitchen.

To carry on this tradition, my solution is to make only small quantities, and save even more time by using today's kitchen technology! Using a microwave and a food processor, two good jars of curd can be produced in just three minutes' cooking time!

Chocolate & Almond Balls

Makes 24

Keep one week at room temperature in an airtight container. Freeze 3 months.

2 egg whites
125g (4oz/1 cup) ground almonds
150g (5oz/1½ cups) desiccated (dried and shredded) coconut
200g (7oz/scant 1 cup) caster (superfine) sugar
4 level tbsp cocoa
2 tsp liquid honey

These have a wonderful, rich chocolate flavour. Don't be tempted to bake the biscuits longer than recommended – when cool, they should be moist on the inside and firm on the outside.

1. Preheat the oven to 200°C (400°F/Gas 6).

2. Whisk the egg whites until they hold firm peaks.

3. Put the ground almonds, 75g (3oz/1 cup) of the coconut, the caster sugar and the cocoa in a bowl and stir well together.

4. Add to the whites with the honey and mix to a soft paste.

5. With wetted palms, roll into balls the size of a small plum.

6. Dip into the remaining coconut and arrange 5cm (2″) apart on baking trays lined with silicone paper.

7. Bake for 8–10 minutes, until the coconut is lightly browned.

8. Remove from the oven and leave on the baking trays for 5 minutes to cool and firm up.

9. Using a knife or spatula, carefully lift on to a cooling tray and store in an airtight container when quite cold.

Cinnamon Balls

Makes about 22   (photograph between pages 120 and 121)

Keep 1 week at room temperature in an airtight container. Freeze 3 months.

If you make only one Pesach biscuit, this one is a prime candidate!

1. Preheat the oven to 160°C (325°F/Gas 3) and lightly oil a baking tray.

2. Beat the egg whites until they form stiff peaks. Stir in all the remaining ingredients, mixing until even in colour.

3. Form into balls with wetted hands and arrange on the baking tray.

4. Bake for 20 minutes or until just firm to the touch.

5. Roll in icing (powdered) sugar while warm and then again when cold.

2 egg whites
125g (4oz/½ cup) caster (superfine) sugar
225g (8oz/2 cups) ground almonds
1 level tbsp cinnamon

For coating the biscuits:
a small bowl of icing (powdered) sugar

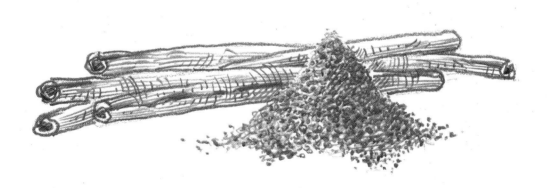

139

Coconut Pyramids

Makes about 16-18   (photograph between pages 120 and 121)

Keep 1 week at room temperature in an airtight container. Freeze 3 months.

2 eggs
125g (4oz/½ cup) caster
    (superfine) sugar
juice and rind of half a
    lemon
225g (8oz/2⅔ cups) fine,
    unsweetened, desiccated
    (dried and shredded)
    coconut

Coconut Pyramids

Many recipes for these traditional biscuits are based on
egg whites, but the use of
whole eggs combined with the
lemon flavouring gives them a
particularly juicy taste and
texture.

However, if you have egg
yolks leftover from recipes
calling for egg whites alone,
you can substitute four of
them for the whole eggs.
However, you may need to use
a little extra lemon juice to get
the correct texture.

These should be slightly moist inside, crunchy on the outside.
If the mixture seems too soft to hold its shape, stir in a little
more coconut.

1. Preheat the oven to 190°C (375°F/Gas 5).

2. Beat the eggs and sugar until creamy, then stir in the lemon
   juice, rind and coconut.

3. Form into cone shapes, most easily done by using an egg cup
   moistened inside with cold water to prevent sticking. As they
   are shaped, turn out on to a baking tray, oiled or lined with
   silicone paper.

4. Bake for 18–20 minutes, until tinged with golden brown.
   Don't overcook!

5. Use a spatula to remove to a cooling tray.

Choco-Walnut Kisses

Makes about 20   **(photograph between pages 120 and 121)**

Keep 1 week in an airtight container. Freeze 3 months.

A crispy meringue biscuit, with a mouth-watering combination of flavours.

1. Preheat the oven to 180°C (350°F/Gas 4). Arrange 20 paper cases on a baking tray.

2. Whisk the egg whites until they form soft peaks when the whisk is withdrawn. Add the sugar a tablespoon at a time, whisking until the mixture stands in stiff peaks after each addition. Whisk in the vanilla and salt.

3. Fold in the coarsely chopped nuts and the cubed chocolate.

4. Fill the paper cases two-thirds full with the mixture and bake for 20 minutes until crisp to the touch and golden.

5. Allow to go cold, then store in an airtight container.

2 egg whites
125g (4oz/$\frac{1}{2}$ cup) caster (superfine) sugar
1 tsp vanilla extract
$\frac{1}{4}$ tsp salt
125g (4oz/1 cup) walnuts, coarsely chopped
125g (4oz) plain (semi-sweet) or milk (sweet) chocolate, cut into roughly 5-mm ($\frac{1}{4}$-inch) cubes

Coconut Macaroons

Makes about 2 dozen

Keep 1 week in an airtight container. Freeze 3 months.

175g (6oz/2⅔ cups) desiccated (dried and shredded)
coconut, toasted
2 large egg whites
125g (4oz/½ cup) icing
(powdered) sugar, sifted
1 tsp vanilla extract

Optional:
125g (4oz) plain (semi-
sweet) or milk (sweet)
chocolate, melted

Toasting the coconut is what gives these little mouthfuls their special 'ta'am' (taste).

1. Preheat the oven to 140°C (275°F/Gas 1) and line a baking tray with silicone paper.

2. Toast the coconut under the grill (broiler) until golden, stirring once or twice – watch it carefully!

3. Whisk the egg whites until they hold floppy peaks, then add the icing (powdered) sugar, a tablespoon at a time, whisking after each addition until stiff peaks form. Stir in the vanilla and the coconut.

4. Put little mounds of the mixture about 5cm (2″) apart on the prepared baking tray.

5. Bake for 20 minutes until the macaroons are set and crispy on top but barely coloured – they will still be moist inside.

6. Transfer to a rack and allow to cool.

Optional:
7. Melt the chocolate in a bowl set over (but not touching) barely simmering water. Alternatively, break up and put it into a small basin and microwave on 100 per cent power for 1½ minutes, then stir till liquid.

8. Dip the bottom of each baked macaroon in the melted chocolate and leave to set. Store in an airtight container.

Passover Kichels

Makes about 4 dozen

Keep 4 days at room temperature in an airtight container. Freeze 1 month.

A good economical family biscuit.

1. Preheat the oven to 190°C (375°F/Gas 5).

2. Line flat baking trays with foil or silicone paper.

3. By hand or machine, mix all the ingredients together (except the jam) until a soft smooth dough is formed.

4. Take pieces of the dough and roll into balls about 2.5cm (1 inch) in diameter, then arrange 5cm (2″) apart on the trays.

5. Dipping the little finger into some cake meal to prevent sticking, make little indentations in each ball and fill with a little jam.

6. Bake for 20 minutes, until pale gold and set.

2 eggs
175g (6oz/¾ cup) caster (superfine) sugar
125g (4oz/½ cup) very.soft or melted margarine
150g (5oz/1¼ cups) cake matzah meal
1 tbsp potato flour
1 tsp grated lemon rind
2 tsp lemon juice
jam

Passover Kichels

It's worth experimenting with your favourite all-the-year round biscuits recipes to make a Passover version, by substituting equal weights of cake matzah meal and potato flour for the ordinary flour (so for 225 g/8oz/2 cups flour, use 125 g/4oz/1 cup cake matzah meal and 125 g/4oz/1 cup potato flour). The texture may not be as fine as with flour, but the biscuits will still be very edible!

Luscious Chocolate Brownies

Makes 24

Keep 1 week in an airtight container. Freeze 3 months.

3 eggs
125 ml (4 floz/½ cup) oil
200g (7oz/scant 1 cup) caster (superfine) sugar
1 tsp vanilla extract
scant 50g (2oz/½ cup) cake matzah meal
25g (1oz/¼ cup) cocoa powder
50g (2oz/½ cup) chopped walnuts

For decoration:
caster (superfine) sugar

The moist squares have a rich chocolate flavour.

1. Preheat the oven to 180°C (350°F/Gas 4). Lightly grease a tin or foil container measuring approx. 27.5 x 17 x 2.5cm (11 x 7 x 1 inch).

2. By hand or machine, whisk together the eggs, oil, sugar and vanilla until slightly thickened and no grains of undissolved sugar can be felt.

3. Sift together the matzah meal and cocoa, and stir into the first mixture until smooth and creamy, then stir in the chopped walnuts.

4. Spoon into the tin or foil container and smooth level, then bake for 25 minutes or until firm to gentle touch. (Overbaking will ruin the lovely moist texture.)

5. Place the tin on a cooling tray, leave for 10 minutes, then sprinkle an even layer of caster sugar over the top of the cake.

6. Cut into squares when cold.

Banana & Almond Sponge with a Cinnamon Streusel Topping

Makes 24 pieces

Keep 1 week in the refrigerator. Freeze 2 months.

An excellent 'cut and come again' cake with a fruity flavour, which matures after 24 hours.

To make the streusel:

1. In a small bowl, mix together the matzah meal, sugar and cinnamon. Stir in the melted fat and mix with a fork or the fingers until crumbly, then stir in the chopped walnuts.

To make the cake:

2. Preheat the oven to 180°C (350°F/Gas 4). Grease a tin or foil container measuring 22.5 x 30 x 5cm deep (9 x 12 x 2″).

3. Mash the bananas with a fork.

4. With an electric whisk, whisk the yolks until they lighten in colour and thicken. Then add the lemon juice, lemon rind and sugar and continue to whisk until the mixture flows in a continuous ribbon when the whisk is lifted.

5. Stir in the mashed bananas, salt, cake matzah meal and ground almonds.

6. Whisk the egg whites until they hold peaks that bend when the whisk is withdrawn. Stir a quarter of this meringue into the banana mixture to lighten the texture, then fold in the remainder very gently, using a rubber spatula.

7. Turn the mixture into the prepared tin or foil container and smooth level.

8. Scatter evenly with the streusel.

9. Bake for 45 minutes or until a skewer comes out clean from the middle and the top springs back to gentle touch.

10. Leave on a cooling rack; when it is cold, leave it in the tin or foil container but cover with foil.

For the streusel topping:
75g (3oz/¾ cup) matzah meal
125g (4oz/1 cup) granulated sugar
1 tsp ground cinnamon
75g (3oz/⅓ cup) melted margarine or butter
75g (3oz/¾ cup) finely chopped walnuts

For the cake:
3 medium bananas
7 eggs, separated
2 tbsp lemon juice
finely grated rind of 1 lemon
275g (10oz/1¼ cups) caster (superfine) sugar
pinch of salt
125g (4oz/1 cup) cake matzah meal
125g (4oz/1 cup) ground almonds

Caramelized Pineapple & Frangipane Tarte

Serves 8–10

Baked case keeps 2 days in the refrigerator. Fill and finish up to 24 hours before serving.
The sweet almond filling makes a delectable contrast to the tart pineapple.

1 x 24–25cm
(9½–10-inch)
part-baked tarte case (see
Tarte au Citron, p. 156)

For the filling:
75g (3oz/¾ cup) ground
  almonds
75g (3oz/⅓ cup) caster
  (superfine) sugar
75g (3oz/⅓ cup) unsalted
  butter or margarine, softened
1 egg
few drops of almond extract
2 level tbsp potato flour

For the topping
1 large pineapple
25g (1oz/2 tbsp) soft unsalted butter or margarine
50g (2oz/¼ cup) caster
  (superfine) sugar
2 tbsp Passover brandy or
  orange liqueur

1. Make and bake the tarte case as for the Tarte au Citron, and allow to cool.

2. Turn the oven down to 180°C (350°F/Gas 4).

3. By hand or machine beat all the filling ingredients together until smooth, then spread evenly on the bottom of the cooled pastry shell and bake for 15 minutes.

4. Meanwhile peel and core the pineapple. Cut into 1cm (⅜-inch) thick rings, then halve them. In a heavy frying pan melt 25g (1oz/2 tbsp) of the fat with the sugar, stirring until the mixture is smooth, and cook the pineapple slices for 8 minutes in it, turning them once carefully, until tinged with gold.

5. Transfer the slices with a slotted spoon to the tarte, arranging them decoratively.

6. Add the liqueur or brandy to the pan and bubble the mixture until it thickens slightly. Brush the pineapple slices with this glaze.

7. Bake the tarte for 10–15 minutes, or until both the crust and the pineapple are golden.

8. Leave to cool on a rack. Serve at room temperature.

One-Stage Chocolate Gateau with Fudge Frosting

Keeps 1 week at room temperature in an airtight container

Freeze 3 months.

A light yet moist and quickly made cake. The fudge frosting can be omitted and the cake sprinkled thickly with icing sugar.

1. Preheat the oven to 180°C (350°F/Gas 4). Lightly oil a 24cm (9½-inch) tin and line the base with a circle of silicone paper.

2. Put all the cake ingredients into a bowl and beat by hand or machine until smooth and creamy – 3 minutes by hand, 2 minutes by electric mixer, 15 seconds by food processor – scraping down the sides halfway through with a rubber spatula.

3. Turn into the prepared tin, level the surface, then bake for 40 minutes until the surface is spongy to a gentle touch.

4. Take out of the oven, leave for 5 minutes, then turn out on to a cooling tray.

To make the frosting:
5. Put the cocoa, liqueur and instant coffee into a small bowl and pour on the boiling water, mixing until smooth.

6. Cream the fat until like mayonnaise, then add the icing (powdered) sugar in two portions, alternately with the cocoa mixture, beating until fluffy.

7. When the cake is completely cold, mix the toasted almonds with the frosting, then spread over the top and sides, forking it into a design.

For the cake:
75g (3oz/¾ cup) cake matzah meal
75g (3oz/½ cup) potato flour
2 tsp Passover baking powder
175g (6oz/¾ cup) caster (superfine) sugar
3 tbsp cocoa
1 tsp vanilla extract
3 eggs
175 ml (6 floz/¾ cup) oil

For the fudge frosting:
2 tbsp cocoa
1 tbsp Sabra or other coffee or chocolate-flavoured liqueur
2 tsp instant coffee
1½ tbsp boiling water
125g (4oz/½ cup) butter or margarine
225g (8oz/2 cups) sifted icing (powdered) sugar
50g (2oz/½ cup) chopped toasted almonds

French Chocolate Cake

Makes one 20cm (8-inch) cake

Keeps 1 week at room temperature in an airtight tin. Freeze 3 months.

125g (4oz/½ cup) unsalted
butter
125g (4oz/½ cup) caster
(superfine) sugar
175g (6oz) plain (semi-
sweet) chocolate
4 yolks
1 tsp vanilla extract
1 tsp Passover baking
powder
50g (2oz/⅓ cup) potato flour
4 egg whites
pinch of salt

For decoration:
icing (powdered) sugar

French Chocolate Cake

You can make this wonderful cake – also known as Queen of Sheba Cake – at any time of the year, but it comes into its own at Passover – it uses only potato flour and contains ground almonds!

Identical recipes for this fabulous cake reached me by way of Paris – from a non-Jewish Parisian cook and a Sephardi one who originally came from Cairo. I haven't been able to discover its actual birthplace, but it's an interesting example of the migration of recipes.

It's the combination of chocolate and potato flour which accounts for its meltingly tender texture.

This superb cake stays moist till the last crumb.

1. Preheat the oven to 180°C (350°F/Gas 4). Grease the inside of a 20cm (8-inch) round loose-bottomed cake tin and line the bottom with a circle of silicone paper.

2. In a small pan, melt the butter, then add the sugar and broken-up chocolate and melt gently together until smooth (or cook in a small basin for 2 minutes on 100 per cent power in the microwave, stirring once).

3. Stir in the egg yolks, vanilla, baking powder and the potato flour.

4. Put the egg whites into a large bowl with a pinch of salt and whisk until they hold stiff, glossy peaks, then use a rubber spatula to fold them gently but thoroughly into the chocolate mixture until the colour is even.

5. Pour the cake mixture into the prepared tin and bake for 40–45 minutes, or until firm to a gentle touch.

6. Leave the cake, still in the tin, on a cooling rack for 5 minutes, then carefully ease out and leave until cold.

7. Sprinkle generously with icing sugar before serving.

Chocolate Roulade with a Mixed Berry Filling

Serves 8–10

Freeze 3 months.

A very special dessert for the Seder.

1. Preheat the oven to 180°C (350°F/Gas 4). Use silicone or greased greaseproof (wax) paper to line a rectangular (roulade) tin measuring 35 x 25cm (14 x 10") across the base and 2.5–4cm (1–1½") deep, mitreing the corners to make a neat fit.

2. Break the chocolate into a small basin and melt it over a pan of simmering water or in a microwave (2 minutes on 100 per cent power, stirring once). Stir in the hot water.

3. Separate the eggs, putting the yolks into a small bowl and the whites into a large one. Add the sugar to the egg yolks and whisk until the consistency of double (leary) cream.

4. Whisk the egg whites until they hold stiff but still glossy peaks.

5. Stir the melted chocolate into the egg yolk and sugar mixture, then stir in a large tablespoon of the meringue.

6. Pour this chocolate mixture down the side of the bowl containing the beaten whites, then use a rubber spatula to fold the two together until the colour is even.

7. Pour this fluffy mixture into the tin and spread it evenly – particularly in the corners.

8. Bake for 20 minutes or until a skewer comes out clean from the centre of the cake.

9. While it is baking get ready a cooling tray, two sheets of greaseproof or silicone paper rather larger than the baking tin, a dry tea (dish) towel and a sifter of icing sugar.

For the roulade:
175g (6oz) plain (semi-sweet) chocolate
2 tbsp hot water
5 eggs
175g (6oz/¾ cup) caster (superfine) sugar
icing (powdered) sugar in a sifter

For the filling:
225g (8oz) frozen mixed berries, defrosted
2 level tbsp caster (superfine) sugar
150 ml (5 floz/⅔ cup) double (heavy) or non-dairy cream

Chocolate Roulade

The secret of success for this flour-less cake is to keep it soft and rollable by covering it the minute it comes out of the oven with paper and a tea (dish) towel to keep in the steam. There will be a little cracking as you roll it up, but not enough to spoil the appearance.

**Chocolate Roulade with a
Mixed Berry Filling**
continued

10. Remove the cake tin from the oven, put on to the cooling tray, and cover lightly first with one sheet of the paper and then the tea towel. Leave to go cold.

11. Meanwhile, prepare the filling. Mix the defrosted fruit with the sugar and leave for 30 minutes. Then whisk the juice that has come out of it together with the cream until thick, and fold in the berries.

12. When the cake is quite cold, turn it out on to a sheet of greaseproof paper, thickly dusted with icing sugar. Peel away the baking paper with care.

13. Spread the cake with the filling and roll up with the help of the sugared paper. Carefully transfer to a serving dish.

14. For ease in cutting this fragile roulade, freeze. Before serving, leave at room temperature for 30 minutes.

Passover Plava

Keeps 1 week at room temperature in an airtight tin. Freeze 3 months.

An all-purpose sponge with a very fine texture.

1. Preheat the oven to 180°C (350°F/Gas 4)

2. Separate the yolks from the whites.

3. Divide the sugar into two equal quantities. Put one quantity of sugar into a bowl with the yolks and whisk until thick and white. (If an electric beater is not available, stand the eggs and sugar in a bowl over a pan of very hot water and whisk until thick and white.) Beat in the lemon juice.

4. In another bowl, whisk the whites until they form floppy peaks. Then beat in the remaining quantity of sugar a table-spoonful at a time until a firm meringue is formed. Fold into the first mixture.

5. Finally, fold in the sifted matzah meal and potato flour.

6. Spoon into the cake tin, which has been oiled and then sprinkled with sugar. Level the surface of the mixture. Sprinkle a thin layer of caster sugar over the top.

7. Bake the 22.5cm (9-inch) cake for 1 hour 10 minutes, the 17cm (7-inch) cake at the same temperature for 45 minutes, until the top is firm to gentle touch.

For 1 x 22.5cm (9-inch) cake:
5 eggs
275g (10oz/1¼ cups) caster (superfine) sugar
1 tbsp lemon juice
75g (3oz/¾ cup) cake matzah meal
75g (3oz/½ cup) potato flour

For 1 x 17cm (7-inch) cake:
3 eggs
175g (6oz/¾ cup) caster (superfine) sugar
2 tsp lemon juice
50g (2oz/½ cup) cake matzah meal
50g (2oz/⅓ cup) potato flour

For sprinkling on top of the cakes:
caster (superfine) sugar

Passover Plava

This beautiful cake is known as a Plava – Russian for sponge – by some Ashkenazim, Pan d'Espana by Moroccan Jews and Pan di Spagna by Italian ones. All the recipes are virtually identical, and I believe this cake dates back to the Golden Age in Spain and is probably of Moorish origin.

Passover Chiffon Sponge

Keep 1 week in an airtight container. Freeze 3 months.

75g (3oz/½ cup) potato flour
65g (2½oz/scant ¾ cup) cake
  matzah meal
150g (5oz/⅔ cup) caster
  (superfine) sugar
5 eggs, separated
50 ml (2 floz/¼ cup) oil
50 ml (2 floz/¼ cup) orange
  juice
1 tsp grated lemon rind
1 tsp grated orange rind
pinch of salt
50g (2oz/¼ cup) caster
  (superfine) sugar

Note: A 25cm (10-inch) angel cake tin works wonderfully well. The finest Passover sponge I know. The small amount of oil helps keep it moist for days.

1. Preheat the oven to 160°C (325°F/Gas 3). Unless using a non-stick angel cake tin, grease and then dust with cake matzah meal a 23–25cm (9–10-inch) ring tin, about 7.5cm (3″) deep.

2. Sift the potato flour, cake matzah meal and the 150g (5oz/⅔ cup) caster sugar into a large bowl and mix well.

3. Separate the eggs and put the whites into a large bowl and the yolks into a small bowl. Mix the oil, orange juice and lemon and orange rinds with the egg yolks. Make a well in the middle of the dry ingredients, pour in the egg-yolk mixture and stir with a wooden spoon until smooth and evenly mixed.

4. Whisk the egg whites with a pinch of salt until they hold stiff, glossy peaks. Then whisk in the 50g (2oz/¼ cup) caster sugar, a tablespoonful at a time, whisking after each addition.

5. Spoon a heaped tablespoon of this meringue on top of the first mixture and mix it in to lighten it. Then spoon the remainder of the meringue on top and, using a rubber spatula, gently but thoroughly fold the two mixtures together.

6. Spoon into the prepared tin, smooth level, then bake for 1¼ hours for a 22.5cm (9-inch) tin, 55 minutes for a 25cm (10-inch) angel cake tin, until firm to a gentle touch.

7. Put the cake, in the baking tin, on a cooling rack and leave until it feels cool to the touch. Loosen from the edges of the tin with the tip of a knife and gently ease out.

Passover Fairy Cakes

Makes 18–20

Keep 1 week in an airtight container. Freeze 3 months.

Spongy and light. Ideal for snacking!

1. Preheat the oven to 200°C (400°F/Gas 6). Arrange 20 paper cases in bun tins or on flat baking trays.

2. Put all the ingredients into a bowl and beat by hand or machine until a smooth batter is formed.

3. Half-fill the paper cases with the mixture.

4. Bake for 15–20 minutes or until golden brown. Cool on a wire rack.

150g (5oz/⅔ cup) soft margarine
175g (6oz/¾ cup) caster (superfine) sugar
3 eggs
140g (4½oz/¾ cup) potato flour
40g (1½oz/6 tbsp) cake matzah meal
1½ tsp Passover baking powder
1 tsp vanilla extract

Variation No.1
Lemon Fairy Cakes

Omit the vanilla, and instead stir in the grated rind of 1 lemon.

Make a lemon icing with 175g (6oz/¾ cup) icing (powdered) sugar mixed with 1 tbsp lemon juice and up to 1 tbsp water (the mixture should be thick enough to coat the back of a spoon).

Spoon a little over each cake and allow to set.

Variation No. 2
Raisin Fairy Cakes

Stir 4 tablespoons raisins into the plain fairy cake mixture.

Layered Apple Torte

Makes I x 24cm (9?1/2-inch) torte. Cuts into 12 generous portions

Will keep 3 days in the refrigerator. Freeze 3 months.

For the filling:
3 very large baking apples
3 tbsp granulated sugar
1 tsp cinnamon

For the cake:
3 eggs
200g (7oz/scant 1 cup) caster (superfine) sugar
175 ml (6 floz/¾ cup) oil
1 tsp vanilla extract
75g (3oz/½ cup) potato flour
75g (3oz/¾ cup) cake
   matzah meal
1½ tsp Passover baking powder

To scatter on top:
granulated sugar

A juicy apple filling is surrounded by a delicate sponge. Special as either a cake or a dessert.

1. Preheat the oven to 180°C (350°F/Gas 4). Grease a 22.5–24cm (9–9½-inch) spring-form or round loose bottomed tin at least 4cm (1½″ deep.

First prepare the filling:
2. Core and peel the apples and grate them coarsely into a mixing bowl, then add the sugar and cinnamon and mix well together.

To make the sponge:
3. By electric whisk: whisk the eggs and sugar until thick and lemon-coloured, then whisk in the oil and vanilla, followed by the dry ingredients.

4. By large capacity food processor: process the eggs and sugar for 2 minutes. Pour in the oil and vanilla and process until it disappears. Then pulse in the dry ingredients until the mixture is smooth and even.

5. Pour half the sponge mixture into the prepared tin, smoothing it level.

6. Spoon the apple filling on top, patting it into an even layer, then cover with the remainder of the sponge mixture.

7. Sprinkle the top of the sponge mixture with the granulated sugar.

8. Bake for 55 minutes or until well risen and firm to a gentle touch in the centre.

Pesach Peach or Nectarine Hazelnut Crisp

Serves 5–6

Keeps 3 days in the refrigerator. Freeze 3 months.

A quick-to-make but satisfying fruit crumble.

1. Preheat the oven to 190°C (375°F/Gas 5).

2. Put the thickly sliced fruit or the drained canned fruit in a large bowl. Toss with the sugar, potato flour and nutmeg, then sprinkle with the lemon juice and liqueur or orange juice.

3. Turn into a lightly greased oven-to-table dish such as a gratin or lasagne-type dish or a foil container measuring approximately 28 x 20cm (11 x 8″).

4. To make the topping, combine the cake matzah meal, potato flour, ground hazelnuts and sugar, then gently rub in the fat by hand or pulse on a food processor until the mixture is crumbly.

5. Sprinkle in an even layer over the fruit and pat level.

6. Bake for 40–45 minutes, or until the fruit feels tender when pierced with a slim pointed knife and the top is golden brown and crunchy.

7. Serve plain or with parev ice cream. Reheats well, most easily in a microwave.

1kg ($2\frac{1}{2}$ lb) ripe peaches or nectarines, or 2 large cans sliced peaches, drained
50g (2oz/$\frac{1}{4}$ cup) granulated sugar
2 tsp potato flour
$\frac{1}{4}$ tsp ground nutmeg
2 tbsp fresh lemon juice
2 tbsp Passover fruit-flavoured liqueur, or orange juice

For the topping:
40g ($1\frac{1}{2}$oz/6 tbsp) cake matzah meal
40g ($1\frac{1}{2}$oz/6 tbsp) potato flour
75g (3oz/$\frac{3}{4}$ cup) ground hazelnuts
125g (4oz/$\frac{1}{2}$ cup) granulated sugar
75g (3oz/$\frac{1}{3}$ cup) margarine or butter

Peach And Hazelnut Crisp

For an ordinary family meal, use the same crumble topping, but substitute baking apples for the peaches. Peel, core and very thinly slice three large baking apples (approximately 675g (1?1/2 lb) – easiest in a food processor. Arrange in an even layer in the same size baking dish. Scatter with the segments from an unpeeled lemon, and spoon over 4 tbsp orange juice and 1 tbsp lemon juice, then scatter with 50g (2oz/?1/4 cup) granulated sugar. Cover with the topping and bake at 190°C (375°F/Gas 5) for 40–45 minutes, or until the apples feel tender when pierced with a slim pointed knife, and the top is golden brown and crunchy.

Tarte au Citron (Lemon Tarte)

Serves 8–10

Keeps 3 days in the refrigerator. Freeze 1 month.

For the pastry:
150g (5oz/⅔ cup)
   butter or block margarine
75g (3oz/½ cup) potato flour
150g (5oz/1¼ cups)
   cake matzah meal
50g (2oz/¼ cup)
   caster (superfine) sugar
1 egg, beaten
1 tbsp lemon juice
1 tsp water

For the filling:
6 eggs
scant 250g (9oz/1 cup
   + 2 tbsp) caster
   (superfine) sugar
225 ml (8 floz/1 cup)
   double (heavy) cream
finely grated rind and juice
   (7 tbsp) of 3 lemons

*For sprinkling on top of
the tarte:*
icing (powdered) sugar

This has a glorious lemon flavour and silky texture. Small slices suffice. My Passover version of the famous French tarte.

To make the pastry:

1. Put the firm fat (cut into roughly 2.5cm/1-inch chunks) in a food processor with the dry ingredients and pulse 10 times to rub in the fat.

2. Add the beaten egg and liquid and pulse until the mixture is beginning to cling together in little moist balls.

3. Tip out into a bowl, gather into a ball with the fingers and then knead well until smooth and free from cracks.

4. Flatten into a block about 2.5cm (1 inch) thick and chill in the refrigerator for at least 30 minutes (or for up to two days). Have ready a 24–25cm (9½–10-inch) oven-to-table flan dish at least 4cm (1½") deep.

5. On a board lightly dusted with potato flour, roll out the chilled dough 3 mm (ug18> inch) thick.

6. Carefully ease it into the dish, taking a little 'tuck' in it all the way round the bottom edge so that the case is slightly thicker near the bottom than the top (to prevent shrinkage). Trim the pastry level with the dish.

7. Prick the bottom and the sides of the case with a fork, then press a large piece of foil into its shape, completely covering the bottom and sides. Freeze while the oven is heating.

8. Preheat the oven to 190°C (375°F/Gas 5).

9. Bake the pastry case for 10 minutes. Carefully remove the foil, prick the case again if it looks puffy, then return to the oven for a further 5–8 minutes or until a pale gold in colour. Cool on a rack.

10. Turn the oven down to 150°C (300°F/Gas 2).

To make the filling:
11. In a large bowl whisk the eggs with the sugar until smooth and well blended.

12. Put the cream in a bowl and whisk very lightly for 10 seconds until slightly thickened.

13. Whisk the lemon rind and juice into the beaten eggs, then whisk in the cream.

14. Pour the filling into the cooled case. Bake for $1\frac{1}{4}$ hours until golden and firm to gentle touch.

15. Leave the tarte to cool for at least 4 hours.

16. Serve chilled, sprinkled with icing (powdered) sugar.

A Tarte of Mixed Berries in an Almond Custard

Serves 8–10

Cooked tarte keeps 2 days in the refrigerator. Freeze unbaked pastry case only, 3 months.

1 x 24–25cm (9½–10-inch) part-baked tarte case, see Tarte au Citron (p. 156)

For the filling:
3 eggs
150 ml (5 floz/⅔ cup) double (heavy) cream
125g (4oz/½ cup) caster (superfine) sugar
1 tsp vanilla extract
50g (2oz/½ cup) ground almonds
40g (1½oz/3 tbsp) melted butter
450g (1 lb) frozen mixed berries or 350–450g (12oz–1 lb) frozen raspberries

This is a Passover version of the famous Tarte Alsacienne, in which fruit is baked in a rich custard – in this case, almond-flavoured.

The pastry is deliciously short and crisp, but crumbles easily, so it's important to cook the tarte in an oven-to-table dish.

1. Preheat the oven to 190°C (375°F/Gas 5).

2. Make and bake the pastry case as for the Tarte au Citron, and allow to cool.

3. Turn the oven down to 180°C (350°F/Gas 4).

To make the filling:
4. Whisk together by hand or machine the eggs, cream, sugar, vanilla and ground almonds, then add the melted butter and stir or process until evenly mixed.

5. Arrange the fruit in an even layer in the pastry case and gently pour on the almond custard.

6. Bake for 45–50 minutes until the custard is set (it will feel spongy to a gentle touch). Serve warm or at room temperature.

7. May be reheated.

158

A Compôte of Stuffed Prunes & Apricots de Luxe

Serves 8

Keeps 4 days in the refrigerator. Freeze 3 months.

An updated version of an old family favourite.

1. Stuff each prune and apricot with a split almond.

2. Put the strained tea and the wine into a saucepan with the sugar and cinnamon. Bring to the boil, then simmer uncovered for 3 minutes to concentrate the flavour.

3. Add the stuffed fruits, raisins and lemon slices. Cover and simmer for 10–12 minutes or until the fruit is tender and has absorbed much of the syrup.

4. Serve plain or with parev ice cream after a meat meal, and with ice cream or natural yoghurt sweetened with a little honey after a milk meal, accompanied by a slice of sponge cake.

1 x 250g (9oz) pack pitted ready-to eat prunes
1 x 250g (9oz) pack tenderized dried apricots
125g (4oz/1 cup) blanched whole almonds, split or cut in two
300 ml (10 floz/1¼ cups) freshly made tea
300 ml (10 floz/1¼ cups) sweet red wine (e.g. Kiddush wine)
2 level tbsp caster (superfine) sugar
1 tsp ground cinnamon
125g (4oz/¾ cup) raisins
1 lemon, very thinly sliced

Pears Poached in Red Wine

Serves 6–8

Keeps 2 days in the refrigerator. Do not freeze.

6–8 firm pears, preferably
   Conference
300 ml (10 floz/1¼ cups)
   fruity red wine
1 level tbsp demerara sugar
150g (5oz/⅔ cup) granulated
   sugar
2 pieces each of thinly
   pared orange and lemon
   peel, about 1.25cm (½
   inch) wide
1 cinnamon stick
4 cloves
1 tbsp lemon juice
2 tsp potato flour
4 tbsp Passover Crème de
   Cassis or cherry brandy

The pears are delicious served plain or with soured cream or thick yoghurt.

1. Peel the pears, but leave them whole. Cut a tiny slice from the base of each so they will stand up evenly in the serving dish.

2. Choose a pan large enough to hold the pears lying flat on the bottom. Put in the wine, sugar, peels, spices and lemon juice and heat gently until the sugar dissolves, stirring all the time.

3. Add the pears, then top up with enough water to cover them.

4. Bring to the boil, cover and simmer very gently, turning once or twice until the fruit feels just tender when pierced with a sharp narrow knife. This will take about 30 minutes for very hard pears, but start testing after 20 minutes. By this time, the pears will be a beautiful pink colour.

5. Take out with a slotted spoon and arrange in the chosen dish.

6. Bring the cooking liquid to the boil, then bubble until the volume is reduced by half and is of a syrupy consistency, with a pleasing 'winey' flavour.

7. Mix the potato flour with the liqueur, then stir into the syrup. Bubble for about 2 minutes until clear, then strain over the fruit.

8. Chill well, preferably overnight.

Frozen Coffee Liqueur Parfait with a Fresh Pineapple Compôte

Serves 8–10

Freeze 3 months.

No eggs are needed for this delicate ice cream, which is simply meringue pieces folded into flavoured cream. It also works well with non-dairy cream.

To make the meringues:
1. Preheat the oven to 150°C (300°F/Gas 2)

2. Mix the sugar and potato flour together.

3. Whisk the whites until they hold floppy peaks, then add the sugar a tablespoonful at a time, whisking until stiff after each addition.

4. Spoon 5cm (2-inch) individual meringues on to baking sheets lined with silicone paper, leaving 5cm (2″) between them.

5. Put the meringues in the oven and immediately turn the heat down to 140°C (275°F/Gas 1). Bake for 1 hour until crisp to the touch and easy to lift off the paper.

6. Allow to go quite cold, then break into roughly 2.5cm (1-inch) pieces.

7. Meanwhile mix the sugar, coffee and water together, stir in the liqueur or additional coffee mixture and chill.

For the meringues:
175g (6oz/¾ cup) caster (superfine) sugar
1 tsp potato flour
3 egg whites

For the syrup:
2 tsp sugar
1 tbsp instant coffee
2 tsp boiling water
2 tbsp Sabra chocolate-orange liqueur (or a further 1 tbsp instant coffee mixed with 2 tsp sugar and 2 tsp boiling water)

For the parfait:
425 ml (15 floz /scant 2 cups) double (heavy) cream or non-dairy cream

For the compôte:
3 tbsp caster (superfine) sugar
2 tbsp lemon juice
1 pineapple, peeled, cored and cut in small pieces

**Frozen Coffee Liqueur
Parfait with a Fresh
Pineapple Compôte**
continued

8. Whip the cream to the soft peak stage, then whisk in the chilled coffee mixture. Fold in the broken meringues.

9. Spoon either into individual soufflé dishes or into a large decorative glass bowl and freeze for at least 48 hours to allow the flavours to develop fully.

10. To make the compôte, dissolve the sugar in the lemon juice over gentle heat. Then pour over the pineapple and chill well.

11. To serve: the parfait is soft enough to serve straight from the freezer. Serve together with the pineapple compôte.

Lemon Bombe with a Strawberry Sauce

Serves 8–10

Freeze 3 months.

The clean, fresh taste of lemon makes this an outstanding ice-cream, happily partnered with a strawberry sauce.

1. Put the juice and finely grated lemon rind into a bowl.

2. Put the egg whites into a bowl with the pinch of salt, then whisk until they hold stiff peaks when the beaters are withdrawn.

3. Add the 75g (3oz/⅓ cup) sugar a tablespoonful at a time, beating until stiff after each addition.

4. Gently whisk in the egg yolks until the colour is even.

5. Put the cream and the remaining caster sugar into another bowl and whisk until it starts to thicken. Then add the lemon juice and rind and whisk until the mixture is thick enough to hang on the beaters when they are lifted from the bowl.

6. Carefully fold in the egg yolk mixture.

7. Turn the ice-cream into a 1.5-litre (2½-pint/6-cup) mixing bowl and leave to freeze for 24 hours.

8. Several hours before it is required, fill a plastic bowl with hot water. Loosen the ice-cream from the edge of the mixing bowl using a sharp knife, then stand in the hot water and count to three slowly. Immediately turn out the bombe on to a serving dish.

9. Put back into the freezer until required.

10. To make the sauce, whirl the fruit, sugar and lemon juice in a food processor until puréed – about 2 minutes.

5 tbsp lemon juice
  (2 lemons)
finely grated rind of
  1 lemon
3 eggs, separated
pinch of salt
75g (3oz/⅓ cup) caster
  (superfine) sugar
extra 25g (1oz/2 tbsp) caster
  (superfine) sugar
300 ml (10 floz/1¼ cups)
  double (heavy)
  or non-dairy cream

For the strawberry sauce:
450g (1 lb) strawberries,
  hulled
50g (2oz/¼ cup)
  caster (superfine) sugar
1 tbsp lemon juice

Lemon Bombe

Dishes containing raw or lightly cooked eggs should not be served to the very young, the elderly, the sick or to pregnant women.

Shavuot
The Feast of Weeks – Pentecost

Among the several reasons given for serving dairy dishes at
Shavuot, I favour the one in the following story. When
Moses came down from Mount Sinai with the God-given
Law, he found the men of Israel dancing round and worshipping
the Golden Calf. However, their womenfolk, whose jewellery
had been snatched by their menfolk to make it, refused to join
in this act of idolatry. As a reward for their conduct, Moses
decreed that they need only make a simple dairy dish rather
than a time and labour-consuming one made with meat.

Obviously Moses didn't have much experience of cooking, or
he would have known that making the favourite Shavuot delicacy – the cheese blintze – demands far more time and skill than
throwing some meat into the pot! Of course, at this period, several thousands of years ago, the women of Israel would have celebrated this Festival with nothing more complicated than delicious Crispy Cheese Pancakes – made in those days with coarse
meal and home-made soft cheese (kaes).

All the wonderful cheesecakes, both sweet and savoury, the
knishes (little savoury pastries) and the strudels are made to
include soft cheese which symbolizes the unblemished Law
given to Moses.

But cheese blintzes, however labour-intensive, still mean
Shavuot in many households, so I have given three versions.
The problem with blintzes is that he or she who fries them isn't
free to sit down at the table with the rest of the family and
guests, as the dedicated cook knows that to reach perfection
they should be eaten hot off the pan. However, I have provided
two innovative recipes – one where pancakes are laid on top of
each other, separated by a delicious cream cheese filling, and
one where they are rolled, but then baked, and served with a
superb cherry sauce.

In Sephardi homes, a harder-pressed cheese such as
Kashkaval, Kefothyi or Parmesan, is likely to feature in such
dishes as Syrian 'bugacho' (a savoury baklava), Turkish 'boreks'
(turnovers) and Greek 'spanakopita' (a filo and spinach bake).

The only reason I can see for the lack of these harder
cheeses in the Ashkenazi cuisine is that they were rarely made

in Eastern Europe, but were much more common in the Ottoman Empire, where the majority of Sephardi communities were established after the expulsion from Spain and Portugal. Yet both the hard-pressed and the soft cheeses are equally rich in the symbolism of Shavuot, representing the purity of the Torah and the harvest of Spring.

A dish that I came across in Alsace seems to me to act as a bridge between the past and the future. 'Bibelaskaes' combines a dish of kaes studded with herbs similar to the one served at Israeli kibbutz breakfasts, accompanied traditionally by sauté potatoes, but equally delicious with crisp (low-fat) crackers.

But Shavuot, called the Feast of Weeks because it occurs seven weeks after the end of Pesach (Passover), is also known as the Time of the Giving of the Law. It is one of the three Pilgrim Festivals and it marks the Time of the Gathering of the First Ripe Fruits. So it's an occasion for celebration as well as prayer, by filling the house and the synagogue with plants and flowers. A poetic reason given is that the Sinai Desert and in particular the area round Mount Sinai where Moses was given the Ten Commandments is normally barren, but suddenly it burst into flower at that first Shavuot. The Book of Ruth is read at this time, and in thanksgiving for the harvest, it is customary to fill the house with the perfume of baking.

Lithuanian Plum Soup

Serves 6- 8

Keeps 3 days under refrigeration. Freeze for 3 months.

1.4kg (3 lb) red stewing plums, stones (pits) removed
140g (4½oz/generous ½ cup) sugar
¼ tsp vanilla extract
350ml (12 floz/1½ cups) any fruity red wine
625ml (22 floz/2¾ cups) cold water
1 cinnamon stick
300ml (10 floz/1¼ cups) soured cream, creamy fromage frais or Greek yoghurt

Lithuanian Plum Soup

If the plums are not free-stone, it helps in the stoning (pitting) process to first microwave them on 100 per cent power for about 5 minutes, or until – when one is cut in half – the stone has begun to separate from the flesh. The same effect will take 20 minutes, covered, in a moderate oven. Be careful – the plums may be very hot in the centre.

The amount of sugar needed will depend on the tartness of the fruit – I give an average amount. It's best to wait until the soup has had a few hours in the refrigerator for the flavours to blend before deciding whether or not it needs more sweetening.

Is it a starter or is it a dessert? What is certain is its rich, mouth-watering taste which makes it the Litvak equivalent of Hungarian Cherry Soup.

1. Put the stoned (pitted) plums in a soup pan together with the sugar, vanilla, wine, water and cinnamon stick. Bring to the boil, stirring to ensure the sugar has dissolved, then cover and simmer very gently for 45 minutes to 1 hour, or until the plum flesh has separated from the skin.

2. Allow to cool to room temperature. Discard the cinnamon stick.

3. Now the contents of the soup pan have to be puréed, but without the plum skins. The quickest way to do this is with a 'moulin à légumes' (a vegetable mill). Otherwise, tip the contents of the soup pan into an ordinary sieve and use a wooden spoon to push down hard on the fruit, leaving the skins behind.

4. Chill the plum purée for a minimum of 3 hours, though overnight is preferable – the flavour develops miraculously during the chilling process.

5. To finish, put about two-thirds of the soured cream or fromage frais into a small bowl. Using a batter whisk or small balloon whisk, whisk in about 300 ml (10 floz/1¼ cups) of the purée until the mixture is an even colour, then add to the remainder of the soup and whisk again. The finished soup should have the texture of thin cream – add a little extra wine if it is too thick.

6. Keep refrigerated until it is served.

7. To serve, top each serving with a little of the remaining cream or fromage frais.

Bibelaskaes with Sauté Potatoes

Serves 6–8

The cheese dip keeps 3 days in the refrigerator.
Serve the sauté potatoes hot off the pan.

This dish from Alsace makes a delicious starter or light supper. If you prefer, omit the sinfully delicious sauté potatoes and serve with brown rolls or digestive biscuits.

1. Mix together the cheese and smetana, fromage frais or yoghurt – the mixture should be light and creamy. Add the remaining ingredients and chill well for several hours, to allow the flavours to blend and mature.

2. Scrub the potatoes, then cook them whole in their skins, covered with boiling salted water, for 25–40 minutes (depending on their size) until absolutely tender when pierced to the centre with a slim pointed knife.

3. Drain the potatoes and return to the empty pan to dry off on a low heat. Leave until cool enough to handle, then skin and cut into thick slices or 2cm (¾-inch) cubes.

4. To fry, put the oil and butter or margarine in a heavy frying pan. When the butter starts to foam, put in the potatoes, and cook very gently, shaking the pan occasionally so that the potatoes absorb the fat rather than fry in it. This will take about 15 minutes.

5. When the potatoes are golden all over, increase the heat to make them crisp. Drain from the fat (there should be very little, if any, left), then put in a dish and sprinkle with salt and black pepper. Serve with the cheese mixture.

6. For a buffet or informal family meal, serve the cheese dip in a bowl. For a more decorative presentation, put on individual glass plates and garnish with leaves of endive or Little Gem lettuce and tiny sprigs of the fresh herbs used.

450g (1 lb) curd or any low-fat soft cheese (e.g. quark)

150ml (5 floz/⅔ cup) smetana, 8 per cent fromage frais or Greek yoghurt

1 red or yellow pepper (bell pepper), deseeded and finely diced

3 fat spring onion (green onion) bulbs, plus 10cm (4″) of the green stem, finely sliced

1 level tsp salt

1 rounded tbsp mixed chopped fresh herbs (e.g. parsley, chives, and tarragon)

1 crushed clove of garlic

For the sauté potatoes:
1.2kg (2½ lb) good frying potatoes (e.g. Maris Piper, Estima, Desirée)

salt

2 tbsp flavourless ground nut (peanut) or sunflower (canola) oil

50g (2oz/¼ cup) butter or margarine

black pepper

Savoury Cheesecake with Olives & Anchovies

Serves 8 (photograph between pages 120 and 121)

Serve the same day. Leftovers keep 2 days in the refrigerator. Do not freeze.

For the pastry:
125g (4oz/1 cup) plain
  (all-purpose) brown flour
125g (4oz/1 cup) plain
  (all-purpose) white flour
½ tsp salt
2 tsp icing (powdered) sugar
1 tsp freeze-dried Herbes de
  Provence
1 rounded tbsp chopped
  parsley
1 tsp dry mustard powder
150g (5oz/⅔ cup) butter or
  block (baking) margarine
1 egg, beaten with 1 tsp
  wine vinegar or cider vinegar and 1 tbsp cold water

For the filling:
350g (12oz/1½ cups) curd
  (low- to medium-fat))
  cheese
3 tsp cornflour (cornstarch)
4 egg yolks, plus 1 whole egg
225ml (8 floz/1 cup)
  whipping cream
1 tsp grated lemon rind
½ teaspoon salt
15 grinds of black pepper
50g (2oz/½ cup) stuffed
  green olives, sliced
1 x 50g (2oz) can of
  anchovies, drained and
  quartered

Based on the 'tarte au fromage blanc' (cream cheese tarte) of Alsace, this makes a superb supper dish for Shavuot. The smooth creamy filling is a mouth-watering contrast to the piquant anchovies and olives.

1. To make the pastry in a food processor, put the dry ingredients, herbs, mustard and the well-chilled fat (cut into 2.5cm/1-inch chunks) into the bowl. Mix the egg, vinegar, and water, then turn on the machine and pour down the feed tube, pulsing only until the mixture looks like a very moist crumble. Then tip it into a bowl and gather together into a dough.

2. Turn the pastry on to a board or counter-top sprinkled very lightly with flour. Knead it gently with the fingertips to remove any cracks, flatten into a 2.5cm (1-inch) thick disc, then wrap in foil or clingfilm (plastic wrap) and chill in the refrigerator for at least 30 minutes.

3. Choose a loose-bottomed flan tin, 22.5–25cm (9–10″) in diameter and 2.5–3cm (1–1¼″) deep. Roll the chilled dough into a circle 27.5–30cm (11–12″) in diameter, then ease into the tin, pressing it well into the sides. Trim off any excess. Prick the case all over with a fork, then line with a piece of foil pressed into its shape.

4. Freeze for 30 minutes.

5. Preheat the oven to 200°C (400°F/Gas 6). Bake the frozen case for 10 minutes or until the pastry feels dry to the touch. Remove the foil and bake for a further 5 minutes until lightly brown, then remove from the oven. Turn the oven down to 190°C (375°F/Gas 5).

6. Meanwhile, make the filling as follows. Put the cheese into a bowl and gradually add the remaining ingredients in the order given (except for the olives and anchovies), using a balloon or hand-held electric whisk to ensure the mixture is smooth. Stir in the anchovies and olives.

7. Pour the filling into the case. Bake for 30 minutes or until puffy and golden, then remove from the oven.

8. Cool for 10 minutes, then serve in wedges.

Savoury Cheesecake with Olives & Anchovies continued

Savoury Cheesecake with Smoked Salmon Topping

Serves 8

Serve the same day. Leftovers keep 2 days in the refrigerator. Do not freeze.

Follow the recipe for savoury cheesecake (p. 168), omitting the olives and anchovies

1. As soon as the cheesecake comes out of the oven, cover with the slices of salmon, drizzle with two generous tablespoons of the yoghurt or soured cream, and sprinkle with the dill.

2. Serve in slices and pass round the remainder of the yoghurt or soured cream.

225g (8oz) best smoked
  salmon, thinly sliced
1 x 250g (9oz/1 cup plus
  2 tbsp) carton Greek
  yoghurt or soured cream
2 tbsp finely snipped dill

Scrambled Eggs with Smoked Salmon & Dill

Serves 6–8 as a starter

Can be served hot off the pan or warm – made just before guests arrive.

12 very fresh eggs,
   preferably free range
   or organic
8 tbsp (approx. 150ml/5
   floz/⅔ cup) crème fraîche
   or extra thick double
   (heavy) cream
¼ tsp sea salt
20 grinds of black pepper
25g (1oz/2 tbsp) butter
1 tbsp fresh snipped dill
175g (6oz) best smoked
   salmon, cut in thin strips
extra dill for garnish
1 brioche, or ciabatta bread
   or challah

This is an informal dish best served to friends who don't mind your absence in the kitchen after they have arrived. Serve it with toasted slices of brioche or ciabatta bread for a starter before a fish main course, or as an unusual 'snack' with a glass of chilled white wine.

It is advisable to cook the scrambled egg in a metal or glass bowl set over a pan filled with 2.5–5cm (1–2″) of boiling water.

1. Whisk the eggs, cream and seasonings together until just blended (I use a hand-held electric whisk).

2. Set the metal bowl over the simmering water, then add the butter. As soon as it has melted, pour in the egg mixture and allow to cook, stirring every now and then with a wooden spoon until the mixture is the consistency of softly whipped cream (as it begins to thicken into curds, you will need to stir it more frequently).

3. As soon as it has reached the required consistency, take from the heat and stir in the dill and smoked salmon. Taste and add more salt if necessary.

4. Serve with the toasted bread.

A Gratin of Fish in a Mushroom & Cream Sauce

Serves 6–8

Serve immediately. Do not freeze.

An inspired combination of flavours in a dish that couldn't be simpler to prepare yet will enchant your guests.

Rolled-up, skinned fillets of plaice may be used instead of the hake.

1. Cook the potatoes in their skins until barely tender. Skin (if necessary) when cool, then slice 1cm ($\frac{3}{8}$ inch) thick.

2. Lightly salt the fish and season the cream with the salt and pepper.

3. Gently sauté the chopped onion in the butter until soft and golden, then add the mushrooms. Stir and continue to cook until there is no free liquid left in the pan. Sprinkle with the nutmeg.

4. Preheat the oven to 160°C (325°F/Gas 3).

5. Take a dish about 4cm ($1\frac{1}{2}$″) deep and wide enough to hold the fish in one layer, and butter it well.

6. Arrange the sliced potatoes evenly over the bottom. Lay the pieces of fish side by side on top and scatter with the sautéed onions and mushrooms. Finally, spoon the seasoned cream over and scatter evenly with the grated cheese. Place a sheet of buttered paper lightly on top.

7. The dish can now be refrigerated for up to 12 hours. Leave at room temperature for 1 hour before baking.

8. Bake for 30 minutes until the sauce is bubbling very slightly and the fish has lost its glassy appearance. Take off the paper and, if the dish is too pale, grill (broil) gently for 3–4 minutes until a rich golden brown.

9. Serve at once.

1kg ($2\frac{1}{4}$ lb) ready-scrubbed new potatoes
6–8 pieces of skinned hake fillet, each approx. 175g (6oz)
salt
pepper
275ml (10 floz/$1\frac{1}{4}$ cups) whipping cream (plus 150ml (5 floz/$\frac{2}{3}$ cup) single (light) cream for 8 people)
1 medium onion, finely chopped
50g (2oz/$\frac{1}{4}$ cup) butter
225g (8oz/2 cups) button mushrooms, thinly sliced
$\frac{1}{8}$ tsp ground nutmeg
6 tbsp grated Cheddar or Gruyère cheese

Baked Blintze Galette

Serves 6–8

Freeze cooked blintzes for 1 month. The oven-ready galette will keep for 1 day in the refrigerator

For the batter:
125g (4oz/1 cup) plain
    (all purpose) flour
2 eggs
25g (1oz/2 tbsp) melted
    butter or 2 tbsp sunflower
    (canola) oil
½ tsp salt
225ml (8 floz/1 cup) milk

For frying the crêpes:
about 2 tbsp of oil

For the filling:
350g (12oz/2 cups) curd (low-
    to medium-fat) cheese or
    quark
175g (6oz/1½ cups) mature
    (sharp) Cheddar cheese,
    grated
1 whole egg, plus 1 egg yolk
3 tbsp chopped fresh herbs
    (preferably parsley,
    dill and chives)
1 tsp salt
15 grinds of black pepper

For the topping:
25g (1oz/2 tbsp) softened but-
    ter
2 tbsp grated Parmesan cheese

To serve:
300ml (10 floz/1¼ cups)
    soured cream or creamy
    fromage frais
Fresh snipped dill

A savoury 'layer cake' of tender crêpes sandwiched with a fresh herb and cheese filling and cut like a cake. A perfect Shavuot dish for today.

1. To make the blintzes, process all the batter ingredients in a blender or food processor until smooth and covered with tiny bubbles – about 30 seconds. Pour into a jug and leave to settle for 10 minutes.

2. Put a teaspoon of oil into a 15cm (6-inch) crêpe or omelette pan and heat until you can feel the heat on your hand held 5cm (2") above it, then wipe out the pan with paper towels.

3. Spoon enough of the batter into the pan to cover the bottom in a thin, even layer. Cook over moderate heat until golden brown underneath, then flip over and cook the second side for about 30 seconds. Turn on to a board covered with silicone or greaseproof (wax) paper. Repeat with the remaining batter, regreasing as necessary.

4. To make the filling, put the cheeses into a bowl, then gradually beat in the egg and egg yolk, followed by all the remaining ingredients. The mixture should be thick but quite spreadable. If not, add a little milk or fromage frais.

5. Preheat the oven to 190°C, (375°F/Gas 5). Butter the inside of a 17cm (7-inch) diameter loose-bottomed cake tin, about 7.5cm (3") deep.

172

6. Lay a blintze on the base of the tin, spoon a heaped table-spoon of filling on top and use the back of the spoon to spread it evenly. Repeat with the remaining blintzes and filling, finishing with a blintze. Spread with the soft butter and scatter with the Parmesan cheese.

7. Cover with foil and bake for 35 minutes. Uncover, turn oven up to 220°C (425°F/Gas 7) and cook for a further 5 minutes to brown the top.

8. Take the tin out of the oven and allow the galette to cool for 5 minutes, then loosen from the sides and stand the tin on a canister of smaller diameter. Pull down the sides and place the galette, still on the base of the tin, on a serving dish.

9. Serve in wedges, accompanied by the soured cream or fromage frais and topped with a little dill.

Cream-Cheese Filled Blintzes with a Sour Cherry Sauce

Serves 6–8

(photograph between pages 120 and 121)

The cooked crêpes will freeze (unfilled) for up to 3 months.

For the filling:
450g (1 lb/2 cups) curd
   (low- to medium-fat)
   cheese
25g (1oz/2 tbsp)
   soft butter
3 tbsp caster (superfine)
   sugar
1 tbsp lemon juice
1 tsp grated lemon rind
$\frac{1}{2}$ tsp vanilla extract
2 tbsp from a 225g
   (8oz/1 cup) carton Greek
   yoghurt (reserve the
   remainder to serve with
   the hot stuffed blintzes)

For the Sour Cherry Sauce:
1 x 425g (15oz) can Morello
   cherries and their juice
3 tsp cornflour (cornstarch)
2 tbsp cherry brandy or
   orange juice
1 tbsp granulated sugar
   (if necessary)

To bake the Blintzes:
25g (1oz/2 tbsp) butter,
   melted

Delicate crêpes are rolled to enclose a sweetened cream cheese filling, baked until golden, then served with a tongue-tingling cherry sauce. This is a legacy from the former Austro-Hungarian Empire.

Crêpes as for Baked Blintze Galette (p.172)

1. To make the filling, combine all the ingredients together and beat until fluffy.

2. To make the sauce, bring the cherries and their syrup to the boil. Stir in the cornflour (cornstarch) mixed with the brandy or orange juice, and allow to bubble for 2 minutes, stirring constantly. Sweeten with sugar if too tart. Pour into a sauce boat and chill.

3. Lay all the crêpes on a board and pipe or spoon a generous tablespoon of the filling across the lower third of each. Turn the sides in and roll up into a cylinder.

4. Arrange side by side on a buttered platter or gratin dish. The blintzes can be refrigerated at this point for up to 24 hours.

5. To bake the blintzes, preheat the oven to 190°C (375°F/Gas 5) and brush the surface of the blintzes with the melted butter. Bake for 15 minutes until golden.

6. Serve accompanied by a spoonful each of cherry sauce and the reserved yoghurt.

Classic Fried Cheese Blintzes

Makes 12. Serves 6–7

Keep ready-to-fry filled blintzes 1 day in the refrigerator.
Freeze 3 weeks. Freeze unfilled blintzes up to 2 months.

The test of a perfect blintze is its paper-thin texture. This is achieved as follows:

1. Put a teaspoon of oil into a 15cm (6-inch) crêpe or omelette pan and heat until you can feel the heat on your hand held 5cm (2″) above it. Then wipe out the pan with paper towels.

2. Instead of pouring into the hot pan only enough batter to fill its base, use a jug to pour a generous amount to cover the base and sides of the hot pan; a very thin layer will set as soon as it touches the base. Immediately pour the excess back into the jug. Very quickly, the blintze will dry on the surface. As soon as the set edges start to curl away from the pan, turn out the blintze, brown-side down, on to a piece of silicone or greaseproof (wax) paper.

3. Regrease the pan as above and then repeat the whole process with the remaining batter. As each cooked blintze stops steaming, pile it on top of the others.

4. To fill the blintzes, place one, brown-side up, on a board and spread it with a tablespoonful of the cheese filling, then turn in the sides and roll up. Repeat with the remaing blintzes.

5. To fry, heat the butter and oil in a heavy frying pan. The minute the butter stops foaming, but before it turns colour, put in the blintzes, join-side up. Cook gently until the underside is golden brown, then turn over carefully and brown the second side.

6. The blintzes can be kept hot and crisp in a low oven, 160°C (325°F/Gas 3) for up to 15 minutes.

7. Serve plain or with well-chilled soured cream or Greek yoghurt.

A marvellous last-minute dish. If you don't have enough cheese

For the classic blintze you will need the same batter as the blintze galette (p. 172), and the same filling as the cream-cheese filled blintzes (p. 174), but without the sauce.

You will also need 50g (2oz/$\frac{1}{4}$ cup) butter and 2 teaspoons of oil for frying the filled blintzes

Fried Blintzes

Little is known about the culinary history of the blintze, but it is thought that the idea of a filled crêpe was brought to Eastern Europe by French chefs, looking for new employment after their aristocratic former employers were caught up in the French Revolution.

However, the method of frying the crêpes seems to be a Jewish notion! Certainly, if you follow my method, your crêpes will truly resemble their Yiddish name of 'bletlach' or skeleton leaf!

Crispy Cream-Cheese Pancakes

Serves 3–4. Serve hot off the pan

225g (8oz/1 cup)
cottage or curd (medium-
to low-fat) cheese
2 eggs
50g (2oz/½ cup)
self-raising flour
(or plain (all-purpose)
flour with ½ tsp baking
powder)
1 level tsp sugar
1 level tsp salt
50g (2oz/¼ cup)
butter or margarine
and 1 tbsp oil
or ⅓ cup oil for frying

*For sprinkling on top of cooked
pancakes:*
2 tsp ground cinnamon
2 heaped tbsp sugar

in the house, add a little more flour. The batter should be thick but liquid enough to drop off a spoon.

1. Put the cheese and the eggs into separate bowls. Beat the eggs with a rotary whisk until fluffy, then stir into the cheese, together with the flour and the seasonings.

2. Put the butter and oil (or the oil) into a heavy frying pan over moderate heat. The minute the butter starts to foam, drop tablespoonfuls of the mixture into the pan, flattening each one slightly with the back of the spoon.

3. Fry gently until risen and golden brown on one side, then turn and cook until the second side is brown.

4. Serve hot off the pan and pass around a mixture of the cinnamon and sugar.

Cream-Cheese Strudel In Soured-Cream Pastry

Serves 12–14

Makes 2 strudels, each about 35cm (14″) long. Keeps 3 days under refrigeration. Freeze 2 months.

The soured cream pastry has a crisp flaky texture that marries brilliantly with the creamy filling.

1. Mix the flour with the fat and rub in, or put it in a food processor and pulse about 5 times until the particles of fat are the size of a hazelnut. Tip into a bowl and mix to a

dough with the soured cream (easiest with your hands, pressing the dough together until evenly moistened) – the bits of
fat should be visible as in rough puff pastry .

2. Divide into two and form each piece of dough into a block
    about 1.25cm ($\frac{1}{2}$" thick. Then wrap each in foil and chill for
    at least 4 hours or overnight. Leave at room temperature for
    20–30 minutes to soften before rolling out.

3. To prepare the filling, beat all the ingredients together until
    the mixture is smooth. This can be done at the same time as
    you make the pastry, and then left to mature with the pastry.

To complete the strudels:
4. Preheat the oven to 200°C (400°F/Gas 6). Have ready two
    ungreased baking trays. Work on one block of chilled pastry
    and half of the filling at a time.

5. Roll the pastry into a very thin rectangle about 40cm (16")
    wide and 22.5cm (9") long – it is very easy to roll. Leaving
    bare the 5cm (2") of pastry nearest to you, arrange the filling
    in a band 5cm (2") wide, leaving 2.5cm (1 inch) of pastry
    bare of filling along each side. Fold in these sides, fold the
    bare pastry nearest to you over the filling, then roll up like a
    flattened Swiss (jelly) roll. You will now have a centre of fill-
    ing surrounded by layers of very thin pastry.

6. Lay the strudel on a baking tray, join-side down.

7. Make another strudel with the remaining pastry and filling
    in the same way.

8. Prick them both all over with a fork. Bake for 10 minutes,
    then turn the heat down to 180°C (350°F/Gas 4) and bake
    for a further 20–25 minutes, or until golden brown. Leave
    for 5 minutes on a cooling tray, then sift an even layer of
    icing (powdered) sugar over the top.

9. To serve, cut into 2.5cm (1-inch) slanting slices.

For the pastry:
175g (6oz/1$\frac{1}{2}$ cups) each
    plain (all-purpose) flour
    and self-raising flour (or
    375g (12oz/3 cups) plain
    (all-purpose) flour with 1$\frac{1}{2}$
    level tsp
    baking powder)
200g (7oz/scant 1 cup) firm
    margarine or butter, cut
    into 2.5cm
    (1-inch) chunks
150ml (5 floz/$\frac{2}{3}$ cup) soured
    cream

For the filling:
450g (1 lb) medium-fat
    curd or full-fat cream
    cheese
25g (1oz/2 tbsp)
    soft butter
1 egg
3–4 tbsp caster (superfine)
    sugar, depending on the
    acidity of the cheese
juice and grated rind of
    half a lemon
1 tsp vanilla extract
1 tbsp cornflour
    (cornstarch)
4 tbsp raisins

For dredging the strudels:
sifted icing (powdered)
    sugar

Cheese Knishes

Makes 24

Keep 2 days under refrigeration. Freeze 3 months raw or cooked.

For the pastry:
225g (8oz/2 cups) plain
 (all-purpose) flour mixed
 with a pinch of salt
1 tsp icing (powdered)
 sugar
150g (5oz/⅔ cup) firm butter
 or block margarine, cut
 into 2.5cm (1 inch) cubes
1 egg
1 tsp vinegar
1 tbsp icy water
extra 25g (1oz/2 tbsp) firm
 butter or margarine

For the filling:
nut of butter
2 fat spring onion (green
 onion) bulbs, plus 10cm
 (4″) of the green stem,
 finely sliced
225g (8oz/1 cup) curd (low
 to medium-fat) cheese or
 sieved cottage cheese
2 tbsp chopped parsley
1 egg, beaten to blend (save
 1 tbsp for the glaze)
1 tsp salt
15 grinds of black pepper
a little soured cream or natural yoghurt

For the glaze:
1 tbsp reserved egg
sesame or poppy seeds

One version of this famous Festival dish uses an egg and oil pastry similar to 'strudelteig' (strudel dough), another a flaky soured-cream dough and a third a noodle dough. Yet another is this rich shortcrust pastry. Although there are many different fillings, at Shavuot one using cheese or savoury mashed potato is always served. The pastry melts in the mouth!

To make the pastry in a food processor:
1. Put the dry ingredients and the cubes of fat into the bowl. Whisk the egg, vinegar and water to blend, then sprinkle over the surface. Put on the lid, then pulse until the mixture is evenly moistened and looks like a crumble. Tip into a bowl and gather into a ball with lightly floured hands.

To make the pastry by hand or in a electric mixer:
2. Sift the dry ingredients into a bowl and add the cubes of fat, then rub in until pieces no larger than a small pea come to the surface when the bowl is shaken. Whisk the egg, vinegar and water to blend, sprinkle over the mixture in the bowl, then mix to a dough.

3. On a floured board, roll the dough mixed by either method into a rectangle about 30 x 15cm (12 x 6″) and spread the top two-thirds with little dabs of the extra 25g (1oz/2 tbsp) of fat. Fold in three, as for flaky pastry. Seal the ends and sides with the rolling pin, then gently flatten and roll out again. Fold in three once more, seal as before, then chill for at least 1 hour or overnight (the dough may also be frozen at this stage).

4. To make the filling, heat the nut of butter and quickly sauté the onions until softened, but not browned.

178

5. Combine with all the other ingredients in a bowl and stir well to blend, adding the soured cream or yoghurt only if necessary – the mixture should be moist, but thick enough to hold its shape.

6. Preheat the oven to 220°C (425°F/Gas 7). Have ready 2 ungreased baking trays.

7. Roll out the chilled pastry 5 mm ($\frac{1}{4}$ inch) thick and cut into 7.5cm (3-inch) rounds with a plain cutter. Put a rounded teaspoon of the filling into the centre of each round, then fold into a half-moon and seal the edges.

8. Arrange on the trays and brush with the beaten egg, then scatter with the sesame or poppy seeds. Bake for 15–20 minutes or until a rich brown. Cool for 15 minutes before serving, or reheat later.

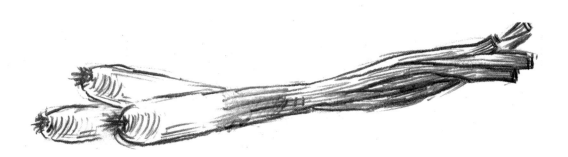

Citrus Cheese Cake with a Kumquat Glaze

Serves 10 (photograph between pages 120 and 121)

Keeps 3 days under refrigeration. Freeze 3 months.

For the crust:
125g (4oz) oat-bake or digestive biscuits
  (graham crackers)
25g (1oz/1 tbsp) melted butter

For the filling:
3 level tbsp pine kernels
  (optional)
450g (1 lb/2 cups) curd cheese
  (low- to medium-fat soft
  cheese) or quark
75g (3oz/⅓ cup) caster sugar
25g (1oz/2 tbsp) softened
  butter
2 level tbsp cornflour
  (cornstarch)
finely grated rind and juice of 1
  large lime
finely grated rind of 1 large
  bright orange
2 tbsp best lime cordial
3 large eggs, whisked to blend

For the topping:
250g (9oz/1 cup + 2 tbsp) carton of creamy (8 per cent)
  fromage frais or soured cream
3 tsp caster sugar
1 tsp lime cordial

For the glazed kumquats:
225g (8oz) kumquats
75g (3oz/⅓ cup) granulated
  sugar
150ml (5 floz/⅔ cup) water

An original combination of flavours makes this a winner. And it's as mouthwatering as it looks!

1. Preheat the oven to 160°C (325°F/Gas 3).

2. Put the pine kernels in the oven for 5 minutes or so to dry during the heating-up process (don't let them colour).

3. Butter the sides of a 20–22cm (8–8½ inch) spring-form tin.

4. Crush the biscuits to crumbs, then mix with the melted butter and press in a even layer on the bottom of the tin.

5. Using an electric mixer or a wooden spoon and a strong right arm (a food processor makes the cheese too pasty), cream the cheese with the sugar and softened butter until fluffy, then mix in the pine kernels, cornflour (cornstarch), grated rinds, juice, cordial and beaten eggs, until smooth and creamy.

6. Turn into the tin and smooth level, then bake for 35–40 minutes until the cake feels set and firm about 2.5cm (1 inch) round the edge of the tin (the remainder of the cake will set as it cools down).

7. Remove from the oven and place on a cooling tray.

8. For the topping, turn the oven up to 200°C (400°F/Gas 6). After 10 minutes, mix the topping ingredients together, then spoon over the cake. Return the cake to the oven and bake for a further 8 minutes.

9. When quite cold, refrigerate for at least 12 hours, preferably overnight.

10. To glaze the kumquats, cut each one into 4 slices, discarding the stalk end.

180

11. Put the sugar and water in a shallow pan 20–22.5cm (8–9″) in diameter and heat gently, stirring, until the sugar is dissolved.

12. Add the kumquat slices in a single layer and let them bubble gently until they are soft and shiny and only about 1 or 2 tablespoons of syrup remain. Leave in the pan until cold (the syrup will set like jam). Use to decorate the top of the chilled cake.

13. Remove the cake from the spring-form tin, but leave it on the base and serve in slices.

Citrus Cheesecake with a Kumquat Glaze

For a cake that's been around since 350 BCE, cheesecake still has amazing vitality – enough to take it into the twenty-first century. Returning recently from the USA with an armful of Jewish cook books, I'm bemused by the sheer inventiveness of such possible masterpieces as Black and White Cheesecake (with bittersweet chocolate), Bialystok Cheesecake (with yeast dough), Italian Cheesecake Puff (with choux pastry and cognac) and 'Lite' Cheesecake (with non-fat cottage cheese, Crème de Cacao and chocolate morsels!).

It was with some trepidation, therefore, that I added to this cornucopia of delights a citrus cheesecake – yet another variation on what started off all those years ago as a confection the ancient Greeks cooked up from goat's cheese and honey.

The trouble is that modern curd cheese is so bland that it needs all the ingenuity of the cook to replace the 'ta'am' (unique taste) of the old style 'kaes' that everybody's grandmother made for Shavuot. This cheese was made by souring milk on the top of the kitchen range until it separated into tangy yet tender curds and whey.

So into plain curd cheese I've stirred the tart, refreshing flavour of fresh limes and the gentler one of orange zest. And if you like your cheesecake plain and simple, just sift icing (powered) sugar over the top.

But there are two further options – choose one or the other, or as I did in my final glorious version, use both. The first is a soured cream topping – if you use creamy (8 per cent) fromage frais, you'll halve the fat content and it works just as well. The second is brand new: Israeli kumquats – with their unique and irresistible sweet-sour flavour – poached in a simple syrup until they turn into shiny golden discs.

However, whichever option you use, do let the cake chill overnight or at least for 12 hours – it vastly improves the flavour and texture and makes portioning much easier.

Cheesecake in a Walnut Crust

Serves 8–10

Keeps 4 days in the refrigerator. Freezes 3 months.

For the crust:
75g (3oz/⅓ cup) firm butter
  or margarine
75g (3oz/⅓ cup) caster
  (superfine) sugar
125g (4oz/1 cup) plain (all-
  purpose) flour
100g (3½oz) pack
  walnut halves

For the filling:
125g (4oz/½ cup)
  butter or soft margarine
75g (3oz/½ cup) caster
  (superfine) sugar
1 tsp vanilla extract
225g (8oz/1 cup)
  cream cheese
225g (8oz/1 cup) curd
  (medium- or low-fat)
  cheese
125ml (5floz/⅔ cup) soured
  cream
  or Greek yoghurt
grated rind of 1 large lemon
2 eggs
50g (2oz/⅔ cup)
  sultanas (white raisins)

The nutty crust adds distinction to this smooth-as-silk cheesecake.

1. Preheat the oven to 220°C (425°F/Gas 7).

2. Lightly oil the inside of a 20–22cm (8–8½ inch) loose-bottomed flan tin at least 4cm (1½″) deep.

3. To make the crust, cut the fat into roughly 2.5cm (1-inch) chunks and put in a food processor with the sugar, then pulse until just combined.

4. Add the flour and pulse until crumbly. Add the walnuts and pulse until the mixture is the consistency of coarse sand.

5. With the fingers, press into the bottom and part-way up the sides of the prepared tin.

6. To make the filling, in an electric mixer (or by hand), beat together the fat, sugar, vanilla and cheese. Add all the remaining ingredients and beat until smooth. Spoon into the unbaked crust.

7. Bake for 10 minutes, then reduce the heat to 180°C (350°F/Gas 4) and bake for a further 20–30 minutes or until the edges are golden and the surface lightly set.

8. Remove to a cooling tray and leave for 30 minutes, then refrigerate still in the tin.

9. To serve, go round the edges of the chilled cake with a sharp knife to loosen it, then remove the side of the tin.

10. Serve the cake whole, or ready-cut in slices or fingers, well-chilled.

Glossary

Ashkenazim	Jews originally of Eastern European origin.
Blintze	A very thin pancake.
Challah (pl. Challot)	An egg and oil-enriched white bread, usually eaten on Shabbat and Festivals.
Charoset	A mortar-like paté of minced nuts, cinnamon and apples.
Chrane	Horseradish and beetroot relish.
Chremslach	Matzah meal pancake.
Eingemacht	Home-made (referring to a sweet preserve).
Etrog(Im)	Citron fruit(s).
Forspeise	Tasty appetiser.
Gefilte	A savoury mixture of minced fish.
Hamantaschen	Three-cornered filled pastry.
Helzel	Stuffing for poultry.
Kaes	Curd cheese.
Kibbeh	A savoury pastry made and filled with bulgur and minced meat.
Kichel	Traditional biscuits.
Kiddush	Prayer over wine usually recited on the eve of Sabbath and Festivals.
Knaidlach	Soup dumplings made with matzah meal.
Knishes	Small savoury pastries.
Kreplach	Meat-filled ravioli, usually served in clear soups.
Kuchen	Light cake traditionally made with yeast
Kugel	A baked casserole dish.
Latkes	A type of potato pancake.
Lekach	Festival cake usually sweetened with honey.
Lokshen	Vermicelli or noodle pasta.
Matzah Meal	Finely-ground matzah.
Matzah	Unleavened bread.
Minhag	A custom or tradition.

Mohn	Poppy seed.
Parev	Neutral – containing neither meat nor milk.
Plava	Very light, fine-textured sponge cake served at Passover.
Rugelach	A rolled up pastry made with curd cheese or sour cream, with a sweet and fruity filling.
Schmaltz	Fat, usually referring to chicken fat or herring, e.g. schmaltz (matjes) herring.
Sephardim	Jews originally from Spain and Portugal.
Shabbat	The Sabbath.
Sufganiyot	Israeli-style doughnuts
Torah	The scroll on which are written the five books of Moses.
Tsimmes	Carrot and meat casserole.
Yomtov	Jewish Festival.

INDEX